What's In A Name?

For your namesake, don't guess! The name you choose for your baby will be a part of his (or her) identity for life. And whether you know it or not, it can affect his personality, popularity or even future business and professional success.

This book is specifically designed to assist you in making your greatest parental decision. Listed here are thousands of boys' and girls' names from which to choose—all alphabetized, all clearly defined. Only you will know the right name for your baby —and somewhere in this book you'll find it.

4000

NAMES

for

YOUR BABY

A DELL BOOK

Published by
DELL PUBLISHING CO., INC.
1 Dag Hammarskjold Plaza
New York, New York 10017

Previous Dell Edition #5709
New Dell Edition

ISBN: 0-440-12709-2

First printing—April 1970
Thirty-first printing—May 1982

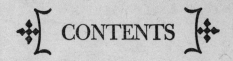

CONTENTS

❦ INTRODUCTION ❧

A Rose
by Any Other Name...

is still a Rose, but if, by chance, Rose's last name were
Budd, Bush or Redd, she would probably daydream of
marriage even more fervently than most other young
girls. Why? Because Rose's parents would have left
their daughter open to years of ridicule and teasing by
ignoring a cardinal rule of naming *any* baby:

*Resist the temptation to be humorous or cute when
matching a baby's given name to his or her surname.*

Fortunately, not many parents surrender to that
temptation (though there *are* birth certificates that read
"Ima Stone" and "Forrest Green"), but, unfortunately,
picking a suitable name for baby isn't simply a matter
of resisting the impulse to be clever. Remember, the
name you choose for your baby will be a part of his
(or her) identity for life; the name you select can affect
your baby's personality and popularity (especially when
he begins school), can color his feelings toward himself,
can even affect the degree of his success in business or
professional life. For example, the name Robin (or
worse, its diminutive form, Rob) Banks would hardly
be an asset to a young man aspiring to a career in
finance or the law.

Be wary of names that are ultra-unique (you and/or baby may tire quickly of such a name) and, especially if baby is a boy, be certain to pick a name that leaves no doubt as to his sex—Jean and Joyce are popular, acceptable names for many European boys, but heaven help any American boy bearing either name!

Listen carefully to the sound and rhythm of the names you're considering for baby. Say the *full* name aloud, letting your ears, good judgment and good taste guide you. Most people find that a surname of just one syllable—Jones, Smith, White, etc.—usually combines best with a given name of two or more syllables. For example, doesn't "Bethany Kent" have a softer, more lyrical sound than "Beth" or "Bess Kent"?

With surnames of two syllables—Carter, Hudson, Turner, etc.—try given names of three syllables, i.e., "Belinda Pauling", Patricia Meaker." And with surnames of three syllables, experiment with given names of one or two syllables, i.e., "Ann Luellen", "Sally Cameron". As you try various names for baby, remember this general rule of rhythm and sound: a full name usually sounds most pleasant when the syllables of the given and surname are *un*equal in number.

Avoid unusual spellings of a name if it makes the name difficult to pronounce. No one wants to go through life hearing his name mispronounced and, perhaps worse, no one wants a name that new acquaintances are hesitant or embarrassed to say aloud. "Jon" is an easy way to vary the spelling of "John" (without changing the name's pronunciation), but you'd be wise not to vary "Alice" by spelling it "Alys"—unless you're unperturbed at the thought of your daughter often being called "Als" or "Alleys".

If your surname is simple, it's usually wise to keep baby's given name simple. You may be drawn to sophisticated names such as Jocelyn or Stephanie, but if your last name is Tead or Stubbs, the combination may sound humorous. In addition, keep in mind the national origin of your surname and of the given names you consider. For example, "Yvonne" and "Jacques" sound fine when combined with a surname such as "DuBrow," but awkward when matched with names such as "Kelly," "Cohen" or "Cappola".

Your religion may affect your choice of baby's name so—*before* you reach a decision—find out if your faith has any specific requirements or traditions regarding the naming of its children. For example, it's traditional that Jewish children are named for a beloved member of the family who is no longer alive, and it's required that Catholic children be given the name of a saint, either as a first or as a middle name. If you have any doubts about the customs or requirements of your faith, talk to your religious leader—*now*.

In this book are more than 3,500 names, plus their origins and their meanings. In order to be able to include as many names as possible, the following form has been used:

CAROLINE: (Teutonic) "one who is strong." Another feminine form of "Charles." Var. and dim., Carola, Carolina, Carolyn, Karolima, Karoline, Karolyn; Carrie, Lina.

Translated, this means that the name "Caroline" is Teutonic in origin, that it means "one who is strong," and that it is one of the many feminine forms of the male name, "Charles." "Carola," "Carolina," "Carolyn," "Karolima," "Karoline," and "Karolyn" are spelling *variants* (abbreviated "var.") of the name "Caroline." Its *diminutives,* which are derivative forms affectionately denoting something small or young (abbreviated "dim.") are "Carrie" and "Lina." Generally, variants are listed alphabetically immediately following

9

the name, and a new alphabetical listing is begun for diminutives.

You will note that many common names are variants or diminutives of another name. "Eleanor" and "Nora," for example, are commonly accepted as names unto themselves. Technically, however, they are both derived from "Helen," since "Eleanor" is a variant of "Helen," and "Nora" is a diminutive of Eleanor.

Many of the names listed in this book are now antiquated; however, their variants and diminutives are often still popular. For example, you aren't likely to name your daughter "Tabitha" or "Tamara," but the diminutive of these names—"Tabbie" and "Tammy"—are names you may want to consider. So, don't skip over any of the names listed, and be sure to check all of the variants and diminutives. Somewhere in the pages of this book is the name that will best suit your precious new baby.

❦[NAMES FOR]❧
Girls

She's made of sunshine, sugar and spice.
She'll be pert and pretty, and awfully nice.
Some day she's bound to change her name—
Now choose the one that will stay the same!

❧[A]❧

ABBEY, ABBIE, ABBY: *see* Abigail.

ABIGAIL: (Hebrew) "a source of joy." Var. and dim., Abbey, Abbie, Abby, Gael, Gail, Gale, Gayl.

ADA: (Teutonic) "joyous," or "prosperous." Var. and dim., Aida, Eda; Addie, Addy.

ADABELLE: "Ada" and "Belle" combined; thus joyous and fair." Var., Adabel.

ADAH: (Hebrew) "ornament."

ADELA, ADELE: *see* Adelaide.

ADELAIDE: (Teutonic) "noble, and of kind spirit." Var. and dim., Adalia, Adaline, Adela, Adele, Adelia, Adelina, Adelind, Adeline, Adella, Adila, Dela, Della; plus all var. and dim. of Ada.

ADELINE: *see* Adelaide.

ADIEL: (Hebrew) "ornament of the Lord." Var. and dim., Adiell, Addie, Addy.

ADINE: (Hebrew) "delicate." Feminine form of Adin. Var., Adena, Adina.

ADNA: (Hebrew) "pleasure." Var., Adnah.

ADORA: (Teutonic) "the beloved; the adored."

ADRIENNE: (Latin) "woman of the sea." Feminine of Adrian. Var., Adria, Adriana, Adriane, Adrianna, Adrianne.

AGATHA: (Greek) "good." Var. and dim., Agathe, Agathy, Ag, Aggie, Aggy.

AGNES: (Greek) "pure, chaste; gentle." Var. and dim.,

13

Agna, Agnella, Agneta, Nessie, Neysa.

AIDA: *see* Ada.

AILEEN: (Greek) "light." Var., Alene, Aline, Eileen, Ilene, Iline, Illene, Illona.

AILSA: (Teutonic) "girl of cheer."

AIMEE: (French) "beloved."

AIRLIA: (Greek) "of the air; ethereal."

✓ **ALANA:** (Celtic) "handsome" or "fair." Feminine of Alan. Var. and dim., Alana, Allana, Alina, Lana, Lane.

ALARICE: (Teutonic) "ruler of all." Feminine of Alaric. Var., Alarise.

ALBERTA: (Teutonic) "noble and brilliant." Feminine of Albert. Var and dim., Albertina, Albertine, Elberta; Bert, Berta, Berte, Bertie.

ALDA: (Teutonic) "rich."

ALDIS: (Old English) "from the oldest house." Var. and dim., Aldas, Aldya; Alda.

ALDORA: (Greek) "winged gift."

ALENE: see Aileen.

ALETHEA: (Greek) "truth." Var. and dim., Aleta, Alitta, Letta.

ALEXANDRA: (Greek) "helper of mankind." Feminine of Alexander. Var. and dim., Alexa, Alexis, Alix, Alla, Elexa, Sandi, Sandra, Sondra.

ALEXIS: *see* Alexandra.

ALFREDA: (Teutonic) "supernaturally wise." Feminine of Alfred. Dim., Ally.

ALICE: (Greek) "truth." Var. and dim., Aleece, Alicia, Alis, Alisa, Alison, Alissa, Allis, Alyce, Alysia, Alyssa, Elissa; Alla, Allie, Ally, Alys.

ALICIA, ALISSA: *see* Alice.

ALIDA: (Greek) "from the city of fine vestments." Var. and dim., Aleda, Alyda, Leda, Lida.

ALISON: *see* Alice.

ALLEGRA: (Latin) "cheerful."

14

ALMA: (Latin) "cherishing."

ALMIRA: (Arabic) "princess; the exalted." Feminine of Elmer. Var. and dim., Elmira, Mira.

ALOYSE: *see* Aloysia.

ALOYSIA: (Teutonic) "famed battler." Feminine of Aloysius. Var. and dim., Aloisia, Aloyse, Lois.

ALTHEA: (Greek) "wholesome; healing." Var. and dim., Altheta, Althee, Thea.

ALVA: (Latin) "white, fair."

ALVINA: (Teutonic) "beloved; friend of all." Feminine of Alvin. Dim., Vina.

AMANDA: (Latin) "lovable." Dim., Manda, Mandy.

AMBER: (Arabic) "jewel."

AMELIA: (Teutonic) "industrious, striving." Feminine of Emil. Var. and dim., Amalia, Amélie, Mell, Mellie, Mill, Millie. *See also* Emily.

AMENA: (Celtic) "honest."

AMY: (Latin) "beloved." Var., Aimée, Ami, Amie.

ANABEL, ANABELLA, ANABELLE: *see* Ann.

ANASTASIA: (Greek) "one who will rise again." Var. and dim., Ana, Stacey, Stacy.

ANATOLA: (Greek) "of the East." Feminine of Anatole.

ANDREA: (Italian) "womanly." Feminine of Andrew. Var. and dim., André, Andreana, Andee, Andi, Andy.

ANGIE: *see* Angela.

ANGELA: (Greek) "heavenly messenger," or "angelic." Var. and dim., Angelica, Angelina, Angeline, Angelita; Angel, Angie, Angy.

ANITA: (Hebrew) "grace." A form (originally Spanish) of Ann. Var., Anitra.

ANN: (Hebrew) "full of grace, mercy and prayer." Originally from the name Hannah. Var. and dim., Anna, Anabel, Anabella, Anabelle, Anne, Annetta, Annette, Annie, Annora, Anya, Nan, Nana, Nancy,

Nanete, Nanette, Nanine, Nanon, Nina, Ninette, Ninon.

ANNETTE: *see* Ann.

ANSELMA: (Teutonic) "the protectress." Dim., Selma.

ANTHEA: (Greek) "like a flower." Var and dim., Anthia; Bluma, Thea, Thia.

ANTOINETTE: *see* Antonia.

ANTONIA: (Latin) "super-excellent." Feminine form of Anthony. Var. and dim., Antoni, Antonina, Antoinetta, Antoinette, Netta, Nettie, Netty, Toinette, Toni.

ANYA: *see* Ann.

APHRODITE: (Greek) "goddess of love."

APRIL: (Latin) "to open" (as the earth opens in spring).

ARABELLA: (Latin) "fair and beautiful altar." Var. and dim., Arabelle; Ara, Bel, Bell, Bella, Belle.

ARDIS: (Latin) "fervent" or "zealous." Var., Ardella, Ardelle, Ardelia, Ardelis, Ardene, Ardine, Ardra.

ARDRA: *see* Ardis.

ARIADNE: (Greek) "holy one." Var., Ariana, Ariane.

ARLENE: (Celtic) "a pledge." Var., Arlana, Arleen, Arlena, Arlette, Arlina, Arline.

ASTRA: (Greek) "like a star." Var., Astrea, Astred, Astrid.

ATHENA: (Greek) "wise; wisdom." Var., Athene.

AUDREY: (English) "strong, noble." Var. and dim., Audrie, Audry; Audie, Dee.

AUGUSTA: (Latin) "majestic, sacred." Feminine of August. Var. and dim., Augustina, Augustine; Austina, Austine, Gusta, Gussie, Tina.

AURELIA: (Latin) "golden." Var., Aura, Aurea, Aurora, Aurelie; Aurel, Aurie, Ora, Orel, Oralia, Oralie.

AURORA: *see* Aurelia.

AVA: *see* Avis.

AVIS: (Latin) "a bird." Var. and dim., Ava, Avi.

AZALIA: (Hebrew) "whom the Lord reserved." Var., Azalea, Azelia.

❦[B]❧

BABETTE: *see* Barbara.

BARBARA: (Greek) "mysterious stranger." Var. and dim., Babette, Barbette; Babby, Babs, Barby, Bobbi, Bobbie.

BATHSHEBA: (Hebrew) "the daughter of our oath." Dim., Sheba.

BEATA: (Latin) "blessed; divine." Dim., Bea.

BEATRICE: (Latin) "she brings joy." Var. and dim., Beatrix; Bea, Bee, Trix, Trixie.

BECKY: *see* Rebecca.

BELINDA: (Italian) "wise and immortal." Dim., Bel, Linda, Lindie, Lindy.

BELLA, BELLE: *see* Isabel.

BENA: (Hebrew) "wise." Var., Benay.

BENEDICTA: (Latin) "one who is blessed." The feminine of Benedict. Var., Benedetta, Benetta, Benita.

BENITA: *see* Benedicta.

BERNADINE: (Teutonic) "brave; strong," The feminine of Bernard. Var. and dim., Bernadette, Bernadina; Berneta, Bernetta, Bernette, Berni, Bernie.

BERNADETTE: *see* Bernadine.

BERNICE: (Greek) "she brings victory." Var. and dim., Berenice; Berni, Berny.

BERTHA: (Teutonic) "shining, bright." Var. and dim., Berta, Bertina, Berti, Bertie.

BERYL: (Hebrew) "jewel; precious." Var. and dim., Beryle; Berri, Berrie, Berry.

BESS, BESSE, BESSIE: see Elizabeth.

BETH: (Hebrew) "place" or "house of God." *See also* Elizabeth.

BETSY, BETTE, BETTINA, BETTY: see Elizabeth.

BEULAH: (Hebrew) "she who will be married."

BEVERLY: (Anglo-Saxon) "beaver-meadow." Var. and dim., Beverley, Beverlie; Bev, Bevvy.

BIANCA, BLANCA: see Blanche.

BILLIE: (Teutonic) "wise protector." A feminine diminutive of William. Var., Bille.

BINA: see Sabina.

BIRDIE: a modern name; "sweet little bird."

BLANCHE: (French) "fair; white." Var., Bianca, Blanca, Blanch, Branca.

BLUMA: see Anthea.

BLYTHE: (Anglo-Saxon) "blithe; happy." Var., Bliss, Blisse.

BOBBI, BOBBIE: see Barbara.

BONNIE: (Latin) "sweet and good." Var., Boni, Bonne, Bonni, Bonny.

BRENDA: (Teutonic) "fiery." Dim., Bren.

BRENNA: (Celtic) "maiden with black or raven hair."

BRIDGET: (Celtic) "mighty; strong." Var. and dim., Bridgid, Brigette, Brigida, Brigitte; Brieta, Brietta, Brita, Brie.

BRIGETTE, BRIGITTE: see Bridget.

BRINA: see Sabrina, Zabrina.

BRUNHILDE: (Teutonic) "heroine on the battlefield." Var., Brunhild, Brunhilda.

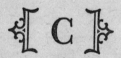

CAMILLA: (Latin) "noble; righteous." Var and dim.,

18

Camella, Camellia, Camille; Cam, Milly.

CAMILLE: *see* Camilla.

CANDACE: (Latin) "pure; glowing fire-white." Var. and dim., Candice, Candida; Candie, Candy.

CARA: (Celtic) "friend."

CARISSA: *see* Charissa.

CARLA: (Teutonic) "one who is strong." A feminine form of Charles. Var. and dim., Karla; Carly, Karly.

CARLOTTA: (Italian) "one who is strong." Another feminine form of Charles.

CARMEL: (Hebrew) "God's fruitful field." Var., Carmela, Carmelita.

CARMEN: (Latin) "a song." Var. and dim., Carmena, Carmina, Carmine, Carmita.

CAROL: (French) "joyous song." Var. and dim., Carole, Carolle, Caryl, Karol, Karole; Carey, Carrie, Cary.

CAROLINE: (Teutonic) "one who is strong." Another feminine form of Charles. Var. and dim., Carola, Carolina, Carolyn, Karolina, Karoline, Karolyn; Carrie, Lina.

CARRIE: *see* Carol, Caroline.

CASSANDRA: (Greek) "the prophetess." Var. and dim., Cassandre; Cass, Cassie.

CATHARINE, CATHERINA, CATHERINE, CATHLEEN: *see* Katherine.

CECILIA: (Latin) "musical." Feminine of Cecil. Var. and dim., Cécile, Cecily, Celia, Cicily, Cis, Cissy.

CELIA: *see* Cecilia.

CELESTE: (Latin) "heavenly." Var., Celesta, Celestine.

CEPORAH: *see* Zipporah.

CHANDRA: (Sanskrit) "she outshines the stars."

CHARISSA: (Greek) "graceful." Var., Carissa.

CHARITY: (Latin) "charitable; loving." Var. and dim., Charita; Charry, Cherry.

CHARLENE, CHARLINE: *see* Charlotte.

CHARLOTTE: (Teutonic) "strong; womanly." Another

19

feminine form of Charles. Var. and dim., Carlotta, Charlene, Charline; Carry, Letty, Lotta, Lotte, Lottie, Lotty.

CHARMAINE: (Latin) "little song." Var., Charmain.

CHERIE: (French) "dear one." Var., Cheryl, Sheryl, Sherry.

CHERYL: *see* Cherie.

CHLOE: (Greek) "fresh blooming." Var., Cloe.

CHRISTABEL, CHRISTABELLE: *see* Christine.

CHRISTINE: (Greek) "fair Christian." The feminine of Christian. Var. and dim., Christa, Christiana, Christina, Christabel, Christabelle, Christal, Chrystal, Crystal; Kristiana, Kristina, Kristine, Chris, Chrissie, Chrissy, Teena, Tina, Xina.

CICELY, CIS, CISSY: *see* Cecilia

CINDY: *see* Cynthia.

CLARA: (Latin) "bright; shining." Var., Claire, Clare, Clareta, Clarette, Clarine.

CLARABELLE: (Latin-French) "bright, shining; beautiful." Var., Claribel.

CLAIRE, CLARE: *see* Clara.

CLARISSA: (Latin) "one who will be famous." Var., Clarice, Clarisa, Clarise.

CLAUDETTE: *see* Claudia.

CLAUDIA: (Latin) "the lame" (this meaning has been obscured by time and usage). The feminine of Claud. Var. and dim., Claude, Claudette, Claudina, Claudine, Claudie.

CLEMENTINE: (Latin) "mild; kind; merciful." Feminine form of Clement.

CLEO: *see* Cleopatra.

CLEOPATRA: (Greek) "of a famous father." Dim., Cleo.

CLOE: *see* Chloe.

CLOTILDE: (Teutonic) "famous battle maiden." Var., Clothilde, Clotilda.

COLETTE: (Latin) "victorious." Var., Collette.

COLLEEN: (Irish) "girl." Var., Coleen, Colene.

CONSTANCE: (Latin) "unchanging; constant." Var. and dim., Constantia, Constantina, Constantine; Con, Conni, Connie.

CONSUELA: (Latin) "consolation." Var. and dim., Consuelo; Connie.

CORA: (Greek) "maiden." Var. and dim., Corene, Coretta, Corette, Corinna, Corinne, Correna, Corrie, Corry.

CORAL: (Greek) "from the sea coral." Var. and dim., Koral; Coralie.

CORDELIA: (Celtic) "the sea's jewel." Var. and dim., Cordellia; Delia, Della.

CORINNA, CORINNE: *see* Cora.

CORNELIA: (Latin) "womanly virtue." Feminine of Cornelius. Var. and dim., Cornela, Nelia, Nell, Nellie.

CRYSTAL: *see* Christine.

CYNTHIA: (Greek) "moon goddess." Dim., Cindy, Cyn, Cynth, Cynthie.

⟦ D ⟧

DAGMAR: (Danish) "joy of the land." Dim., Dag.

DAISY: (Anglo-Saxon) "the day's eye." Var., Daisie.

DALE: (Teutonic) "dweller in the valley." Var., Dail, Daile.

DAMARA: (Greek) "gentle girl." Var. and dim., Damaris; Mara.

DAPHNE: (Greek) "laurel tree." Dim., Daph, Daphie.

DARCIE: (French-Celtic) "from the stronghold; dark one." Var., Darcey, Dercy.

DARDA: (Hebrew) "pearl of wisdom." Var., Dara.

DARICE: (Persian) "queenlike." Var. and dim., Da-reece, Darees; Dari.

DARLENE: (Anglo-Saxon) "dearly beloved." Var. and dim., Darleen, Darline, Daryl.

DAVINA: (Hebrew) "the loved." Feminine of David. Var., Daveta, Davida, Davita.

DAWN: (Anglo-Saxon) "the break of day."

DEANNA: *see* Diana.

DEBORAH: (Hebrew) "the bee." Var. and dim., Deb-ora, Debra; Deb, Debbie, Debby.

DEBRA: *see* Deborah.

DEE: *see* Audrey, Deidre, Dorothy.

DEIDRE: (Gaelic) "sorrow." Var. and dim., Dierdre; Dee, Deedee.

DELIA: (Greek) "from the isle of Delos." *See also* Cordelia.

DELILAH: (Hebrew) "the temptress." Var. and dim., Dalila; Lila.

DELLA: (Teutonic) "of nobility." Dim., Del.

DELPHINE: (Greek) "calmness; serenity." Var., Del-phinia.

DEMETRIA: (Greek) "from a fertile land." Var. and dim., Demitria, Dimitria; Demy.

DENISE: (Greek) "wine goddess." The feminine of Dennis. Var., Denice, Denys.

DESDEMONA: (Greek) "girl of sadness." Var. and dim., Desdamona; Demona, Mona.

DESIRÉE: (French-Latin) "so long hoped for."

DIANA: (Latin) "pure goddess of the moon." Var. and dim., Deanna, Diane, Dianna; Di.

DIANE: *see* Diana.

DINAH: (Hebrew) "judged; exonerated." Var., Dina.

DIONE: (Greek) "the daughter of heaven and earth."

DIXIE: (American) "girl of the South." Dim., Dix.

DODI: *see* Doris.

DOLLEY, DOLLIE, DOLLY: *see* Dorothy.

DOLORES: (Latin) "our Lady of Sorrows." Var. and dim., Delores, Deloris, Dolora; Dori, Dorrie, Dorry.

DOMINICA: (Latin) "born on the Lord's day." Feminine of Dominic. Var., Dominique.

DOMINIQUE: *see* Dominica.

DONNA: (Italian) "lady." Var., Dona.

DORA: (Greek) "a gift." *See also* Dorothy, Eudora.

DORENE: (French) "golden girl." Var. and dim., Doreen, Dorine; Dori, Dorie, Dorrie, Dorry.

DORINDA: (Greek) "bountiful gift." Dim., Dori, Dorin.

DORIS: (Greek) "sea goddess." Dim., Dodi.

DOROTHY: (Greek) "God's gift." A feminine form of Theodore. Var. and dim., Dora, Doretta, Dorothea, Dorothi, Dorthea, Dorthy; Dee, Dolley, Dollie, Dolly, Dore, Dot, Dottie, Dotty.

DORRIE, DORRY: *see* Dorene.

DOTTIE, DOTTY: *see* Dorothy.

DRUSILLA: (Greek) "soft-eyed." Var. and dim., Drucilla; Dru, Drus, Drusie.

DULCIE: (Latin) "charming; sweet." Var., Dulci, Dulcine.

EARTHA: *see* Hertha.

EDEN: (Hebrew) "enchanting."

EDIE: *see* Edith.

EDITH: (Teutonic) "rich gift." Var. and dim., Eadith, Eda, Edythe; Eadie, Ede, Edie, Edina.

EDLYN: (Anglo-Saxon) "of nobility." Dim., Lyn.

EDNA: (Hebrew) "rejuvenation." Dim., Edny.

EDWINA: (Anglo-Saxon) "valued friend." Feminine of

23

Edwin. Var. and dim., Eadwina, Eadwine, Edwine; Win Wina, Winnie, Winny.

EFFIE: (Greek) "fair and famed." Var., Effy.

EILEEN: *see* Aileen.

ELAINE: (Greek) "light." Var. and dim., Alaine, Alayne, Elana, Elayne; Laine, Lani.

ELBERTA: *see* Alberta.

ELEANOR, ELEANORA, ELEANORE, ELENORE, ELINOR, ELNORE: *see* Helen.

ELECTRA: (Greek) "shining star." Dim., Lectra.

ELENA: *see* Helen.

ELEXA: *see* Alexandra.

ELFREDA: (Teutonic) "noble and wise." A feminine form of Albert. Var., Elfrida.

ELISE: *see* Elizabeth.

ELISSA: *see* Alice.

ELITA: (Latin) "select; a special person."

ELIZA: *see* Elizabeth.

ELIZABETH: (Hebrew) "consecrated to God." Var. and dim., Elisa, Elisabeth, Elisabetta, Elise, Eliza, Elsa, Elsbeth, Else, Elsie, Lisabet, Lisbeth; Bess, Besse, Bessie, Beth, Betsy, Bette, Betti, Bettina, Betty, Libby, Lisa, Lise, Liza, Lizzie, Lizzy.

ELLA, ELLIE: *see* Helen.

ELLEN: *see* Helen.

ELMA: (Greek) "pleasant."

ELMIRA: *see* Almira.

ELOISE: *see* Louise.

ELSA, ELSIE: *see* Elizabeth.

ELVIRA: (Spanish) "like an elf." Dim., Elva, Elvie.

EMILIA: *see* Emily.

EMILY: (Teutonic) "industrious." A feminine form of Emil. Var. and dim., Emilia, Emilie, Em, Emmy, Millie.

EMMA: (Teutonic) "one who heals." Dim., Em, Emie, Emmie, Emmy.

ENDORA: (Hebrew) "fountain."

ENID: (Celtic) "purity of soul."

ERICA: (Scandinavian) "of royalty." Feminine of Eric. Var. and dim., Erika; Rica, Rika, Ricky, Riki.

ERINA: (Celtic) "girl from Ireland." Var., Erin, Erina.

ERMA: *see* Irma.

ERNESTINE: (Teutonic) "earnest; purposeful." Feminine of Ernest. Var. and dim., Erna, Ernesta, Teena, Tina.

ESMERALDA: (Greek) "emerald." Var. and dim., Ezmeralda; Esme.

ESTELLE: (Latin) "a star." Var. and dim., Estella; Stella.

ESTHER: (Hebrew) "a star." Var. and dim., Esta, Ester; Essie, Essy.

ETHEL: (Teutonic) "noble." Var., Ethyl.

ETTA: *see* Henrietta.

EUDORA: (Greek) "wonderful gift." Dim., Dora.

EUGENIA: (Greek) "well-born." Feminine of Eugene. Var. and dim., Eugenie; Gena, Gene, Genie, Gina.

EUNICE: (Greek) "gloriously victorious."

EUPHEMIA: (Greek) "fair and famed." Var. and dim., Euphemie; Effie.

EURYDICE: (Greek) "broad separation."

EVA: *see* Eve.

EVADNE: (Greek) "fortunate."

EVANGELINE: (Greek) "bearer of good news."

EVE: (Hebrew) "life" or "living." Var. and dim., Eva, Eveleen, Evelina, Eveline, Evelyn, Evita, Evonne; Evie.

EVELYN: *see* Eve.

EVONNE: *see* Eve.

❦[F]❧

FAITH: (Latin) "trusting; faithful." Var., Fae, Fay, Faye.

FANNY: (Teutonic) "free." Var., Fan, Fannie.

FAUSTINA: (Latin) "very lucky." Var., Faustena, Faustine.

FAY, FAYE: *see* Faith.

FELICIA: (Latin) "happy." Feminine of Felix. Var., Felice, Felise.

FERN: (Greek) "a feather."

FIDELA: (Latin) "faithful woman." Var. and dim., Fidelia, Fidella; Fidelity.

FIFI: *see* Josephine.

FIONNA: (Celtic) "ivory-skinned." Var. and dim., Fiona, Phiona, Viona, Vionna; Fio.

FLAVIA: (Latin) "yellow-haired; blonde."

FLEUR, FLEURETTE, FLORA: *see* Florence.

FLORENCE: (Latin) "to flower and bloom." Var. and dim., Fleur, Fleurette, Flora, Florette, Floria, Floris, Flower; Flo, Flossie.

FRANCES: (Teutonic) "free." Feminine of Francis. Var. and dim., France, Francesca, Francine, Fran, Franny.

FREDA: (Teutonic) "peace." A feminine form of Frederick. Var. and dim., Freida, Frida, Frieda; Fredie.

FREDERICA: (Teutonic) "peaceful." Another feminine of Frederick. Var. and dim., Fredrica, Fredrika, Ricky.

FRITZIE: (Teutonic) "peaceful ruler." Feminine of Fritz. Var., Fritzi, Fritzy.

❧[G]❧

GABEY, GABIE: *see* Gabrielle.

GABRIELLE: (Hebrew) "woman of God." Feminine of Gabriel. Var. and dim., Gabriella, Gabey, Gabi, Gabie.

GAIL, GALE: *see* Abigail.

GARNET: (Teutonic) "radiant red jewel."

GAY: (origin uncertain) "merry." Var., Gae, Gaye.

GEMINI: (Greek) "twin." Var., Gemina.

GENA, GENE, GINA: *see* Eugenia, Regina.

GENEVIEVE: (Celtic) "white; pure." Var., Geneva.

GEORGETTE: *see* Georgiana.

GEORGIANA: (Greek): "earth-lover." Feminine of George. Var. and dim., Georgetta, Georgette, Georgia, Georgianna, Georgina, Georgine, Georgi, Georgie.

GERALDINE: (Teutonic) "ruler with a spear." Feminine of Gerald. Var. and dim., Geralda, Jeraldine; Geri, Gerri, Gerry, Jerrie, Jerry.

GERDA: (Teutonic) "the protected." Var. and dim., Garda, Gerdi.

GERTRUDE: (Teutonic) "spear maiden." Dim., Gerta, Gerti, Gertie, Gerty, Trude, Trudy.

GILBERTA: (Teutonic) "the bright pledge." Feminine of Gilbert. Var. and dim., Gilberte; Gilbertine, Gilbertina.

GILDA: (Celtic) "God's servant." Dim., Gilli.

GINGER, GINNY: *see* Virginia.

GISELLE: (Teutonic) "a promise." Var., Gisela, Gisele.

GITTEL: (Hebrew) "maiden of the winepress." Var., Gitel, Gitle, Gittle.

GLADYS: (Latin) "frail; delicate." Var. and dim., Gladine, Gladis; Glad, Gladdie.

GLENDA: *see* Glenna.

GLENNA: (origin uncertain) "from the valley." Feminine of Glenn. Var. and dim., Glenda, Glennis, Glynis; Glen, Glenn, Glennie.

GLORIA: (Latin) "the glorious." Dim., Glory.

GLORIANA, Gloria and Anna combined; thus, "glorious grace." Var., Glorianna.

GLYNIS: *see* Glenna.

GOLDIE: (Teutonic) "the golden-haired one." Var., Goldy.

GRACE: (Latin) "the graceful." Var. and dim., Gracia; Gracie, Gracye.

GREDEL, GRETA, GRETCHEN: *see* Margaret.

GREER: (Greek) "the watchwoman."

GRISELDA: (Teutonic) "the heroine." Dim., Grissel, Selda, Zelda.

GUINEVERE: (Celtic) "fair lady." Var. and dim., Guenevere, Jennifer; Gen, Genny, Jen, Jenni, Jennie, Jenny.

GUSTA: *see* Augusta.

GWENDOLEN: (Celtic) "white-browed." Var. and dim., Gwendolyn; Gwen, Gwenn, Gwyn, Gwyneth, Wendi, Wendy.

GYPSY: (of undetermined origin) "wanderer."

HAGAR: (Hebrew) "one who flees." Var., Haggar.

HANNAH: (Hebrew) "full of grace, mercy and prayer." For var. and dim., *see* Ann.

HAPPY: (a modern name) "a happy child; joyful.

HARRIET: (Teutonic) "mistress of the home." A

feminine of Henry. Var. and dim., Harrietta, Harriette; Hatti, Hattie, Hatty.

HATTIE, HATTY: *see* Harriet.

HAZEL: (Anglo-Saxon) "authority or commander."

HEATHER: (Anglo-Saxon) "a flower." Dim., Heath.

HEDDA: (Teutonic) "war." Var., Hedy, Heddy.

HEDWIG: (Teutonic) "storm; strife." Var. and dim., Hedvig, Edvig; Hedi.

HEIDI: *see* Hilda.

HELEN: (Greek) "light." Var. and dim., Helena, Helene, Hellene, Eleanor, Eleanora, Eleanore, Elena, Elene, Elenore, Elinor, Elinore, Ella, Ellen, Elnore, Lenore, Leonora, Leonore, Leora, Lora, Lorine; Ellie, Lenni, Lennie, Nell, Nellie, Nelly, Nora.

HELGA: (Teutonic) "holy."

HELOISE: *see* Louise.

HELSA: (Hebrew) "given to God."

HENNI, HENNIE: *see* Henrietta.

HENRIETTA: (Teutonic) "mistress of the home." A feminine form of Henry. Var. and dim., Henriette, Henrika; Etta, Etty, Henni, Hennie, Hetti, Hetty.

HEPHZIBAH: (Hebrew) "my joy is in her." Var. and dim., Hepsiba, Hepsibah; Hepsibetha.

HERA: (Greek) "queen of the Gods."

HERMIONE: (Greek) "of the earth." Feminine of Herman.

HERTHA: (Teutonic) "earth mother." Var., Eartha.

HESPER: (Greek) "night star."

HESTER: (Persian) "a star." Dim., Hetti, Hettie, Hetty.

HETTI, HETTIE, HETTY: *see* Henrietta, Hester.

HILARY: (Latin) "cheerful." Var., Hillarey, Hillary.

HILDA: (Teutonic) "battle-maiden." Var. and dim., Heidi, Hilde; Hildie, Hildy.

HILDEGARD: (Teutonic) "battle-maiden." Var. and dim., Hildagard, Hildagarde, Hilde; plus all dim. of Hilda.

HOLLY: (Anglo-Saxon) "good luck." Var., Hollie.

HONEY: *see* Honora.

HONORA: (Latin) "honorable." Var. and dim., Honey, Honoria; Nora, Norah, Noreen, Norine, Norrie.

HOPE: (Anglo-Saxon) "optimistic and cheerful."

HORTENSE: (Latin) "garden worker." Var., Hortensa.

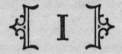

IANTHE: (Greek) "purple-colored flower." Dim., Ian.

IDA: (Teutonic) "happy." Var., Idalla, Idelle.

IDELIA: (Teutonic) "noble."

IDELLE: *see* Ida.

IGNACIA: (Latin) "ardent." Feminine of Ignatius. Var., Ignatia, Ignatzia.

ILENE, ILINE, ILLENE, ILLONA: *see* Aileen.

ILKA: (Celtic) "hard worker."

ILSA, ILSE: var. of Elsa; thus, *see* Elizabeth.

IMOGENE: (Latin) "an image." Var., Imogen.

INA: *see* Katherine.

INEZ: (Greek) "chaste; pure; gentle." Var., Ines.

INGA: *see* Ingrid.

INGRID: (Swedish) "daughter." Var., Inga, Ingeborg.

IONA: (Greek) "purple jewel." Var., Ione, Ionia.

IRENE: (Greek) "peace." Var. and dim., Eirene, Irena, Irina, Renata, Rena, Rene, Reni, Rennie, Renny.

IRIS: (Greek) "rainbow."

IRMA: (Teutonic) "strong." Var. and dim., Erma, Erme; Irmina, Irmine, Irme.

ISABEL: (Hebrew) "consecrated to God." Originally from the name Elizabeth. Var. and dim., Isabella, Isabelle, Isbel, Isobel; Bel, Bella, Belle.

ISADORA: (Greek) "a gift." Feminine of Isidore. Var.

and dim., Isidora; Dora, Dori, Dory, Issy, Izzy.

ISOLDE: (Celtic) "the fair." Var., Isolda.

IVAH: (Hebrew) "God's gracious gift." Var., Iva.

IVY: (origin uncertain) "a plant or a vine."

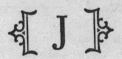

JACINDA: (Greek) "beautiful; comely." Var., Jacenta.

JACQUELINE: (Hebrew) "the supplanter." Feminine of Jacques. Dim., Jackie.

JADA: (Hebrew) "wise." Var., Jadda, Jadah.

JAN: *see* Jane.

JANE: (Hebrew) "God's gracious gift." Feminine of John. Var. and dim., Gianna, Janet, Janette, Janice, Jayne, Jean, Jeanne, Jeanette, Jeannine, Joan, Joana, Joanna, Johanna, Juanita, Gian; Jan, Janey, Janna, Jeanie, Joanie, Jone, Jonie, Juana.

JANET, JANETTE, JANICE: *see* Jane.

JASMINE: (Persian) "fragrant flower." Var., Jasmin, Jasmina, Yasmin.

JEAN, JEANNE, JEANETTE: *see* Jane.

JEANNINE: *see* Jane.

JEMIMAH: (Hebrew) "dove." Var., Jemima, Jemmima.

JENNIE, JENNIFER, JENNY: *see* Guinevere.

JERALDINE: *see* Geraldine.

JERRI, JERRIE, JERRY: *see* Geraldine.

JESSE: *see* Jessica.

JESSICA: (Hebrew) "rich," or "grace of God." Feminine of Jesse. Dim., Jess, Jesse, Jessi, Jessie, Jessy.

JEWEL: (Latin) "a precious stone."

JILL: *see* Julia.

JINNY: *see* Virginia.

31

JO: *see* Josephine.

JOAN, JOANNA: *see* Jane.

JOBINA: (Hebrew) "the afflicted." Var., Jobyna.

JOCELYN: (Latin) "the fair." Var. and dim., Jocelin, Joslyn; Lyn, Lynn.

JODIE: *see* Judith.

JOHANNA: *see* Jane.

JOLIE: (French) "pretty."

JOSEPHINE: (Hebrew) "she shall add." Feminine of Joseph. Var. and dim., Josephina; Fifi, Jo, Josie.

JOY: (Latin) "joy."

JOYCE: (Latin) "joyful."

JUANITA: *see* Jane.

JUDITH: (Hebrew) "admired; praised." Var. and dim., Juditha; Jodie, Jody, Judy.

JULIA: (Greek) "youthful." Feminine of Julius. Var. and dim., Juliana, Juliane; Juliet, Julietta, Juliette, Julie, Jill.

JULIETTE: *see* Julia.

JUNE: (Latin) "young."

JUNO: (Latin) "queen of the Gods."

✓ **JUSTINE:** (Latin) "the just." Feminine of Justin. Var. and dim., Justina; Tina.

K

KAREN, KARIN, KARYN: *see* Katherine.

KARLA: *see* Carla.

KAROL: *see* Carol.

KAROLINA, KAROLINE, KAROLYN: *see* Caroline.

KATE: *see* Katherine.

KATHERINE: (Greek) "pure." Var. and dim., Catherina, Catherine, Cathleen, Karen, Karena, Karin, Karyn, Katharina, Katharine, Katherin, Kathleen,

Kathlene, Kathryn, Katrina; Cassie, Ina, Kara, Kate, Kathie, Kathy, Katie, Kit, Kittie, Kitty, Trina.

KATHLEEN, KATHLENE: *see* Katherine.

KATRINA: *see* Katherine.

KATHY: *see* Katherine.

KAY: (Greek) "rejoice."

KENDRA: (Anglo-Saxon) "the knowing woman."

KIM: (origin uncertain) "noble" or "glorious leader."

KIRBY: (Anglo-Saxon) "from the church town." Var., Kirbee, Kirbie.

KIRSTEN: (Scandinavian) "the anointed one."

KIT, KITTY: *see* Katherine.

KOREN: (Greek) "young girl."

KRISTIANA, KRISTINA, KRISTINE: *see* Christine.

KYLA: (Gaelic) "comely."

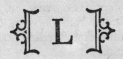

LAINE: *see* Elaine.

LANA: *see* Alana.

LARA: (Latin) "well-known."

LARAINE: *see* Lorraine.

LAURA: (Latin) "the laurel." Feminine of Lawrence. Var. and dim., Laureen, Laurel, Lauren, Laurette, Lora, Loralie, Lorelie, Loren, Loretta, Lorette, Lorinda, Lorine, Lorna, Lorne; Lari, Loree, Lori, Lorie, Lorrie.

LAUREEN, LAUREN: *see* Laura.

LAURETTE: *see* Laura.

LAVERNE: (French) "springlike." Var. and dim., Laverna, LaVerne; Verna, Verne, Vern.

LAVINIA: (Latin) "woman of Rome." Var. and dim., Lavina; Vina, Vinia.

LEAH: (Hebrew) "the weary." Var. and dim., Lea, Leigh; Leda, Lida.

LEANNE: (Anglo-Saxon) combination of Lee and Ann. Var., Liana, Lianne.

LEDA: *see* Alida, Leah.

LEE: (Anglo-Saxon) "meadow." Var., Lea, Leigh.

LEILA: (Arabic) "black" or "dark as the night." Var. and dim., Leilah, Leela, Lee.

LELA, LELAH, LELIA: *see* Lillian, below.

LENA, LINA: a dim. of Helena, Carolina, etc., but used as an independent name.

LEONA: (Latin) "the lion." Feminine of Leo. Var. and dim., Leola, Leone, Leoni, Leonie; Lee, Lennie, Lenny.

LEONORA, LEONORE, LENORE: *see* Helen.

LEONTINE: (Latin) "brave as a lion." Another feminine of Leo. Var., Leontyne.

LESLEY: (Celtic) "from the grey fort." Feminine of Leslie. Var. and dim., Leslie, Lesli, Lesly; Les.

LETA: *see* Letitia.

LETITIA: (Latin) "joy; delight." Var. and dim., Leticia; Leta, Lettie, Letty, Tish.

LETTIE, LETTY: *see* Charlotte, Letitia.

LIBBY: *see* Elizabeth.

LIDA: (Slavonic) "loved by all." Var., Lyda. *See also* Alida, Leah.

LILA, LILAH, LILLA: *see* Delilah, Lillian.

LILLIAN: (Latin) "a lily." Var. and dim., Lela, Lelah, Lelia, Lila, Lilah, Lilia, Lilian, Lilyan; Lil, Lilla, Lilli, Lillie, Lilly, Lily.

LILLIE, LILLY, LILY: *see* Lillian.

LILLITH: (Hebrew) "evil woman; bad wife." Var., Lilith, Lilis.

LILYBELLE: (Latin) "the beautiful lily." Var., Lillibel, Lilybell, plus all dim. of Lillian.

LINDA: (Spanish) "beautiful." A dim. of Belinda, Rosa-linda, etc., but used also as an independent name. Var. and dim., Lynda; Lind, Lindie, Lindy, Lynd.

LISA, LISE, LIZA, LIZZIE, LIZZY: *see* Elizabeth.

LISABET, LISABETH, LISBETH: *see* Elizabeth.

LIVIA: *see* Olivia.

LOIS: (Greek) "battle maiden." A feminine form of Louis.

LOLA: (Spanish) "strong woman." A feminine form of Charles. Dim., Loleta, Lolita.

LOLITA: *see* Lola.

LORA: *see* Laura, Helen.

LORALIE: *see* Laura.

LORELEI: (Teutonic) "lurer to the rocks."

LORETTA: *see* Laura.

LORI, LORIE, LORRIE: *see* Laura.

LORINE: *see* Laura, Helen.

LORNA: *see* Laura.

LORRAINE: (Teutonic) "famous in battle." Var., Laraine, Loraine.

LOTTA, LOTTIE, LOTTY: *see* Charlotte.

LOTUS: (Egyptian) "flower of the lotus tree; bloom of forgetfulness."

LOUISE: (Teutonic) "battle maiden." A feminine form of Louis. Var. and dim., Eloise, Heloise, Louisa; Lou.

LU, LULU: *see* Lucy.

LUBA: (Slavonic) "lover." Var., Lubba.

LUCILLE: *see* Lucy.

LUCRETIA: *see* Lucy.

LUCY: (Latin) "light." Feminine of Lucius. Var. and dim., Lucia; Lucilla, Lucille, Lucinda, Lucie, Lu, Lulu.

LUELLA: (Latin) "the appeaser." Var., Louella.

LUNA: (Latin) "of the moonlight."

LYDIA: (Greek) "cultured." Dim., Liddy.

LYNN: a dim. of Evelyn, Madeline, etc., but used also as an independent name. Var., Lyn, Lynna, Lynne.

LYRIS: (Greek) "of the music of the lyre; lyrical." Var., Liris.

MABEL: (Latin) "amiable; lovable." Var. and dim., Mabelle, Maybelle; Belle, Mae.

MADA: *see* Madeline.

MADELINE: (Hebrew) "a tower of strength." Var. and dim., Madeleine, Madelene, Madelon, Magdalen, Marleen, Marlene, Marline; Mada, Madid, Maddie, Magda.

MADGE: *see* Margaret.

MADRA: (Latin) "mother."

MAE: *see* May.

MAGDA, MAGDALEN: *see* Madeline.

MAGGIE: *see* Margaret.

MAGNOLIA: (Anglo-Saxon) "girl of the magnolia tree."

MAIDA: (Anglo-Saxon) "maiden." Dim., Maidy.

MAISIE: *see* Margaret.

MALINA: (Hebrew) "from a high tower." Var., Melina.

MAMIE: *see* Mary.

MANDA, MANDIE, MANDY: *see* Amanda.

MANON: *see* Mary.

MARA: *see* Damara, Mary.

MARCELLA: *see* Marcia.

MARCIA: (Latin) "of Mars." Feminine of Mark. Var. and dim., Marcella, Marsha; Marcie, Marcy.

MARGARET: (Greek) "a pearl." Var. and dim., Madge, Margarete, Margarita, Margery, Margo, Margot, Marjorie; Gredel, Greta, Gretchen, Mag, Maggie, Maisie, Marge, Margie, Meg, Peg, Peggy.

MARGERY, MARJORIE: *see* Margaret.

MARGO: *see* Margaret.

MARIA: *see* Mary.

MARIAM, MARIAN, MARION: *see* Mary.

MARIE: *see* Mary.

MARIETTA, MARIETTE, MINETTE: *see* Mary.

MARIGOLDE: (Anglo-Saxon) "like the flower marigold." Var., Marigold.

MARILYN: *see* Mary.

MARINA: (Latin) "sea maiden." Dim., Rina.

MARIS: (Latin) "sea star." Var. and dim., Marisa, Marras, Marris, Mari.

MARLA: *see* Mary.

MARLEEN, MARLENE, MARLINE: *see* Madeline.

MARSHA: *see* Marcia.

MARTHA: (Aramaic) "the lady." Var. and dim., Marta, Martella, Marthe, Marti, Martie, Matti, Mattie.

MARTINA: (Latin) "belonging to Mars." Feminine of Martin. Var. and dim., Marteena, Martine; Marti, Teena, Tina.

MARVA: (Latin) "wonderful." Dim., Marvella.

MARY: (Hebrew) "bitter." Var. and dim., Mara, Mari, Maria, Mariam, Marian, Marie, Marietta, Mariette, Marilyn, Marion, Marla, Marya, Maureen, Minette, Miriam, Moira, Morene; Mamie, Manon, Mimi, Mitzi, Mitzie, Moll, Mollie, Molly, Polly.

MATHILDA: (Teutonic) "brave in battle." Var. and dim., Maud, Maude, Matti, Matty, Tilda, Tillie, Tilly.

MAUD, MAUDE: *see* Mathilda.

MAUREEN: *see* Mary.

MAURITA: (Latin) "little dark girl." Var. and dim., Mauretta, Morita; Mauri, Rita.

MAVIS: (Celtic) "songbird."

MAXINE: (Latin) "greatest." Feminine of Maximilian.

MAY: (Anglo-Saxon) "kinswoman." Var., Mae.

MEDEA: (Greek) "part goddess; sorceress."

MEG: *see* Margaret.

✓ **MEGAN:** (Celtic) "the strong." Var., Meghan.

MEHETABEL: (Hebrew) "one of God's favored." Var., Mehitable, Metabel.

MELANIE: (Greek) "darkness; clad in black." Var. and dim., Melania, Malan, Melan, Melina, Mel; Mellie, Melly.

MELBA: *see* Melvina.

MELINA: *see* Malina, Melanie.

✓ **MELISSA:** (Greek) "honey bee." Var. and dim., Melisa; Lisa, Mel.

MELODY: (Greek) "song." Var. and dim., Melodie; Lodie.

MELVINA: (Celtic) "chief." Feminine of Melvin. Var. and dim., Malvina; Melba.

MENA: *see* Philomena.

MERCEDES: (Spanish) "merciful." Dim., Merci, Mercy.

MERCY: *see* Mercedes.

MEREDITH: (Celtic) "protector of the sea."

MERLE: (Latin) "the blackbird." Var., Merla, Meryl.

MERRIE: (Anglo-Saxon) "joyous; merry." Var., Meri.

MERRITT: (Anglo-Saxon) "of merit." Dim., Merri.

MERT, MERTA: *see* Myrtle.

MERYL: *see* Merle.

META: (Latin) "ambitious."

MIA: (Latin) "mine."

MIGNON: (French) "dainty."

MILDRED: (Anglo-Saxon) "soft; gentle." Dim., Milli, Millie.

MILLICENT: (Teutonic) "strength." Var. and dim., Melicent, Milicent; Milli, Millie, Milly.

MILLIE, MILLY: *see* Camilla, Emily, Mildred, Millicent.

MIMI: *see* Mary.

MINA: *see* Wilhelmina.

MINERVA: (Greek) "wise." Dim., Min, Minnie, Minny.

MINNA: (Teutonic) "loving remembrance." Dim., Min, Mini, Minnie, Minny.

MINNIE, MINNY: *see* Minerva, Minna.

MIRABEL: (Latin) "of great beauty." Var. and dim., Mirabelle; Mira, Bell, Belle.

MIRANDA: (Latin) "to be admired." Dim., Randie, Randy.

MIRIAM: *see* Mary.

MITZI: *see* Mary.

MODESTA: (Latin) "shy; unassuming." Var. and dim., Modeste; Desta, Deste.

MOIRA: *see* Mary.

MOLLIE: *see* Mary.

MONA: (Latin) "the alone; the peaceful."

MONICA: (Latin) "advisor." Var., Monique.

MORENE: *see* Mary.

MORLA: (Hebrew) "chosen by the Lord."

MORNA: (Gaelic) "the tender and gentle." Var., Myrna.

MURIEL: (Hebrew) "bittersweet." Var. and dim., Meriel, Murielle; Mur.

MYRA: (Latin) "the wonderful," Var., Mira.

MYRNA: *see* Morna.

MYRTLE: (Greek) "victorious crown." Var. and dim., Merta, Myrta; Mert, Myrt.

NADIA: *see* Nadine.

NADINE: (French) "hope." Var. and dim., Nada, Nadia.

NAN, NANCY: *see* Ann.

NANETTE, NINON: *see* Ann.

NAOMI: (Hebrew) "sweet; pleasant." Dim., Nomi.

NARDA: (origin uncertain) "joyous; gay." Var., Nara.

NATALIE: (Latin) "child of Christmas." A feminine form of Nathan. Var. and dim., Natala, Natale, Natalee, Natalia, Natasha, Nathalie, Natica, Natika; Nat, Nattie, Netta, Nettie, Netty.

NATASHA: *see* Natalie.

NEDA: (Slavonic) "Sunday's child." Var. and dim., Nedda, Neda, Nedi.

NELDA: (Old English) "of the elder tree."

NELL, NELLIE, NELLY: *see* Cornelia, Helen.

NERINE: (Greek) "nymph of the sea." Var. and dim., Nereen, Nerin, Nerina.

NERISSA: (Greek) "of the sea." Var., Nerita.

NESSIE, NEYSA: *see* Agnes.

NETTA, NETTIE: *see* Antonia, Natalie.

NICOLE: (Greek) "victory of the people." Feminine of Nicholas. Var. and dim., Nichola, Nicola, Nicolette, Nikola; Niki, Nikki.

NINA, NINETTE: *see* Ann.

NOEL: (Latin) "a Christmas child." Feminine of Noel. Var., Noella, Noelle.

NOLA: (Celtic) "famous; well-known." Feminine of Nolan.

NOLL, NOLLIE: *see* Olivia.

NONA: (Latin) "ninth born." Var. and dim., Nonna, Nonie.

NORA, NORAH: *see* Eleanor, Helen, Honora.

NOREEN, NORINE, NORRIE: *see* Honora.

NORMA: (Latin) "the model" or "pattern." Feminine of Norman. Dim., Normi, Normie.

NYDIA: (Latin) "a refuge."

❦[O]❧

OCTAVIA: (Latin) "the eighth born." Feminine of Octavius. Dim., Tavia, Tavi.

ODELE: (Greek) "a melody." Var., Odel, Odelet, Odell.

ODELIA: (Teutonic) "prosperous." Var., Odella, Odile.

ODETTE: (French) "home lover," or "little patriot." Var., Odet, Odetta.

OLA: (Scandinavian) "daughter" or "descendant." The feminine of Olaf.

OLGA: (Teutonic) "holy."

OLIVIA: (Latin) "the olive." Feminine of Oliver. Var. and dim., Olive; Livi, Livia, Livvi, Noll, Nollie, Nolita, Olli, Ollie.

OLIVE: *see* Olivia.

OLYMPIA: (Greek) "of the mountain of the Gods."

ONA, OONA: *see* Una.

ONDINE: *see* Undine.

OPAL: (Sanskrit) "jewel."

OPHELIA: (Greek) "wise," or "immortal." Dim., Phelia.

ORA, ORALIA, ORALIE, OREL: *see* Aurelia.

ORIBEL: (Latin) "of golden beauty." Var. and dim., Orabel, Orabelle, Oribelle; Ori.

ORIOLE: (Latin) "fair; flaxen-haired." Var., Oriel.

✓ **ORLENA:** (Latin) "the golden." Var., Orlene, Orlina.

ORNA: (Irish) "olive-colored."

OTTILIE: (Teutonic) "battle heroine." Var. and dim., Otila, Ottillia; Otti, Ottie, Uta.

{ P }

PAIGE: (Anglo-Saxon) "child" or "young." Var., Page.

PAMELA: (origin uncertain) "loving; kind." Dim., Pam.

PANDORA: (Greek) "talented; gifted." Dim., Dorie.

PANSY: (Greek) "fragrant; flower-like." Var., Pansie.

PAT: *see* Patricia.

PATIENCE: (Latin) "patient."

PATRICIA: (Latin) "of the nobility; well-born." Feminine of Patrick. Var. and dim., Patrica, Patrice; Pat, Patsy, Patti, Patty, Tricia, Trish.

PATSY: *see* Patricia.

PAULA: (Latin) "little." Feminine of Paul. Var. and dim., Paulette, Paulina, Pauline, Paulita; Pauli, Paulie.

PAULINE: *see* Paula.

PEARL: (Latin) "precious gem." Var. and dim., Pearle, Perle, Perl; Perlie.

PEG, PEGGY: *see* Margaret.

PEGEEN: (Celtic) "pearl."

PENELOPE: (Greek) "weaver." Dim., Pen, Pennie, Penny.

PENNY: *see* Penelope.

PEONY: (Greek) "flower." Var., Peonie.

PEPITA: (Spanish) "she shall add." Dim., Pepi, Peta.

PERDITA: (Latin) "lost."

PERLE: *see* Pearl.

PETRA: (Greek) "rock." Feminine of Peter. Var. and dim., Peta, Petta; Pet, Pete.

PETRINA: (Greek) "steadfast; resolute." Feminine of Peter. Var. and dim., Petra, Petrine; Peti, Petie.

PETUNIA: (Latin) "for the petunia flower."

PETULA: (Latin) "peevish one." Var. and dim., Petulah; Pet.

PHELIA: *see* Ophelia.

PHENICE: (Hebrew) "from a palm tree." Var., Phenica, Phenicia.

PHILANA: (Greek) "friend of mankind." Var., Philina, Philine, Phillane.

PHILIPPA: (Greek) "lover of horses." Feminine of Philip. Var. and dim., Philipa, Philippe, Pippa.

PHILOMENA: (Greek) "loving friend." Dim., Mena.

PHOEBE: (Greek) "the wise, shining one." Var., Phebe.

PHYLLIS: (Greek) "a green bough." Var. and dim., Philis, Phillis, Phylis; Phyl.

PIA: (Italian) "devout."

PIERRETTE: (French) "steady." Feminine of Pierre.

POLLY: (Hebrew) "bitter." Dim., Pol, Poll, Pollie. *See also* Mary.

POMONA: (Latin) "fertile."

POPPY: (Latin) "fragrant."

PORTIA: (Latin) of uncertain meaning. Var., Porcia.

PRIMA: (Latin) "first born."

PRIMROSE: (Latin) "the first rose." Dim., Rose, Rosie.

PRISCILLA: (Latin) "the ancient; of long lineage." Var. and dim., Prisilla; Pris, Prissie, Prissy, Sil.

PRUDENCE: (Latin) "the prudent; cautious." Dim., Pru, Prud, Prudi, Prudie, Prudy.

PSYCHE: (Greek) "the soul."

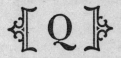

QUEENA: (Teutonic) "a queen," or "a woman."

QUEENIE: see Regina.

QUENBY: (Scandinavian) "wife; womanly."

QUERIDA: (Spanish) "loved one."

QUINTA: (Latin) "the fifth child." Var., Quintina.

QUIRITA: (Latin) "citizen."

❦[R]❦

RACHEL: (Hebrew) "naive and innocent; like a lamb." Var. and dim., Rachele, Rachelle, Rochelle; Rae, Ray, Shelley.

RAE, RAY: see Rachel.

RAMONA: (Teutonic) "protector." Feminine of Raymond. Dim., Mona, Rama.

RANA: (Sanskrit) "of royalty." Var. and dim., Rania, Rani.

RANDY: see Miranda.

RAPHAELA: (Hebrew) "blessed healer." Feminine form of Raphael. Var., Rafaela.

REBA: see Rebba, Rebecca.

REBBA: (Hebrew) "the fourth born." Var., Reba, Rebah.

REBECCA: (Hebrew) "the captivator." Var. and dim., Rebekah; Reba, Riba, Riva, Becky.

REGINA: (Latin) "queenly." Var. and dim., Regan, Regine; Gina, Gine, Queenie, Reggie.

RENA: see Irene.

RENÉE: (French) "reborn." Var. and dim., Renata, Reni, Rennie.

RHEA: (Greek) "motherly."

RHODA: (Greek) "a garland of roses." Dim., Rodi, Rodie.

RICKY: dim. of Erica, Frederica, Roderica, etc.

RITA: (Greek) "a pearl." A dim. of Norita, Margarita, Clarita, etc., but used also as an independent name.

RIVA: *see* Rebecca.

ROANNA: (Latin) "sweet; gracious." Var., Roana, Roanne.

ROBERTA: (Anglo-Saxon) "of shining fame." Feminine of Robert. Var. and dim., Robina, Ruberta, Ruperta; Bobbe, Bobbi, Bobbie, Robin, Robina, Robi, Robbi, Robbie.

ROBIN, ROBINA: *see* Roberta.

ROCHELLE: *see* Rachel.

RODERICA: (Teutonic) "ruler" or "princess." Feminine of Roderick. Dim., Rica.

ROLANDA: (Teutonic) "famed." Feminine of Roland. Dim., Ro, Rola.

ROMA: (Latin) "the wanderer," or "woman of Rome."

RONALDA: (Teutonic) "powerful." Feminine of Ronald. Dim., Rona, Ronnie, Ronny.

RONNIE, RONNY: *see* Ronalda, Veronica.

ROSA: *see* Rose.

ROSABEL: (Latin) "beautiful rose." Var., Rosabella.

ROSALIE: *see* Rose.

ROSALIND: (Latin) "fair rose." Var. and dim., Rosalinde, Roselyn, Roslyn, Rosalyn; Ros, Roz.

ROSAMOND, ROSAMUND: *see* Rose.

ROSANNE: (Latin) "gracious rose." Var., Rosanna, Rosann.

ROSE: (Latin) "a rose." Var. and dim., Rosa, Rosalee, Rosaleen, Rosalia, Rosalie, Rosamond, Rosamund, Rosena, Rosene, Rosetta, Rosel, Rosella, Roselle, Rosette, Rosie, Rosina, Rosita, Rozina, Rozalie.

ROSEMARIE: (Latin) "Mary's rose." Var., Rosemary.

ROSENA: *see* Rose.

ROWENA: (Celtic) "flowing white hair." Dim., Ro.

ROXANE: (Persian) "dawn." Var., Roxana, Roxanna, Roxanne; Rox, Roxie, Roxy.

RUBY: (Latin) "precious red stone." Var., Rubetta.

RUTH: (Hebrew) "a beautiful friend." Dim., Ruthie.

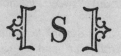

SABINA: (Latin) of uncertain meaning. Var. and dim., Sabine, Savina; Bina.

SABRINA: (Anglo-Saxon) "a princess." Dim., Brina.

SACHA: (Greek) "helpmate."

SADIE, SADYE: *see* Sarah.

SALENA: (Greek) "salty."

SALLIE, SALLY: *see* Sarah.

SALOME: (Hebrew) "a woman of perfection."

SAMANTHA: *see* Samuela.

SAMARA: (Hebrew) "watchful; cautious." Dim., Mara.

SAMUELA: (Hebrew) "name of God." Feminine of Samuel. Var. and dim., Samella, Samuella; Sam, Samantha.

SANDRA, SANDY: *see* Alexandra.

SAPPHIRE: (Greek) "beautiful jewel."

SARAH: (Hebrew) "princess." Var. and dim., Sadye, Sara, Sarena, Sarene, Saretta, Sari, Shari, Sharon, Sarita, Sadie, Sal, Sallie, Sally.

SARETTA, SARITA: *see* Sarah.

SELENA: (Greek) "the moon." Var. and dim., Salene; Lena.

SELMA: (Celtic) "the fair."

SERAPHINE: (Hebrew) "ardently religious." Var. and dim., Serafina, Sera.

SERENA: (Latin) "tranquil."

SHARON: (Hebrew) "of the land of Sharon." Var. and dim., Shara, Shari.

SHEBA: *see* Bathsheba.

SHEILA: (Celtic) "musical." Dim., Shelley.

SHELLEY: *see* Rachel, Sheila.

SHERYL, SHERRY, SHERI: *see* Cherie, Shirley.

SHIRLEY: (Anglo-Saxon) "from the white meadow." Var. and dim., Sheryl, Shirlee, Shirlie; Sherry, Sheri, Shirl.

SIBYL: *see* Sybil.

SIDNEY, SIDONIE: *see* Sydney.

SILVANA: *see* Sylvia.

SILVIA: *see* Sylvia.

SIMONE: (Hebrew) "heard by the Lord." Feminine of Simon. Var., Simonetta.

SONDRA: *see* Alexandra.

SONIA, SONJA, SONYA: *see* Sophia.

SOPHIA: (Greek) "wisdom." Var. and dim., Sofia, Sonia, Sonja, Sonya; Soph, Sophi, Sophie, Sophey, Sophy.

SOPHIE: *see* Sophia.

STACEY: *see* Anastasia.

STARR: (Anglo-Saxon) "star."

STELLA: *see* Estelle.

STEPHANIE: (Greek) "a crown" or "garland." Feminine of Stephen. Var. and dim., Stefanie, Stephana, Stephania, Stephenie; Stevie.

SUSAN: (Hebrew) "a lily." Var. and dim., Susana, Susanna, Susanne, Susannah, Suzanna, Suzetta; Sue, Susi, Susie, Susy, Suzie, Suzy.

SYBIL: (Greek) "the prophetess." Var. and dim., Sibel, Sibell, Sibyl, Sybyl; Sib, Sibie, Sibbie, Sibby.

SYDEL: (Hebrew) "the enchantress." Var., Sydelle.

SYDNEY: (Hebrew) "the enticer." Feminine of Sidney. Var. and dim., Sidney, Sidonia, Sidonie; Sid, Syd.

SYLVIA: (Latin) "forest maiden." Var. and dim., Silva, Silvana, Silvia; Syl, Sylvie.

[T]

TABITHA: (Aramaic) "the gazelle." Dim., Tabbie.

TALLULAH: a modern American name "vivacious." Var. and dim., Tallula; Tallu.

TAMARA: (Hebrew) "the palm tree." Dim., Tama, Tammy.

TAMMY: *see* Tamara.

TANIA: (Russian) "the fairy queen." Var., Tanya.

TARA: (Celtic) "tower."

TAVIA: *see* Octavia.

TEENA, TINA: *see* Christine, Ernestine, etc.

TERESA: (Greek) "the harvester." Var. and dim., Theresa, Thérèse, Tracey, Tracy; Tess, Tessa, Tessie.

TESS, TESSA, TESSIE: *see* Teresa.

THALIA: (Greek) "blooming."

THEA, THIA: *see* Alethea, Althea, Anthea, Theodora.

THEDA: *see* Theodora.

THELMA: (Greek) "nursing."

THEO: *see* Thedora, Theola.

THEODORA: (Greek) "God's divine gift." The feminine of Theodore. Var. and dim., Theodosia; Dora, Dori, Teddi, Teddie, Theda, Thea, Theo, Thia.

THEOLA: (Greek) "heaven sent." Dim., Lola, Theo.

THERA: (Greek) "untamed."

THERESA: *see* Teresa.

THOMASINA: (Hebrew) "the twin." Feminine of Thomas. Var., Thomasa, Thomasine.

THORA: (Teutonic) "thunder."

TILDA, TILLIE, TILLY: *see* Mathilda.

TIMOTHEA: (Greek) "honoring God." Feminine of Timothy.

TINA: dim. of Christine, Ernestine, Martina, etc., but also used as an independent name.

TIPPI, TIPPIE: *see* Zipporah.

TOBEY: (Hebrew) "God is good." Feminine of Tobias. Var. and dim., Tobé, Tobi.

TONI: *see* Antonia.

TRACY: *see* Teresa.

TRILBY: (of uncertain origin) "frivolous; giddy."

TRINA: *see* Katherine.

TRISTA: (Latin) "woman of sadness."

TRIXIE: *see* Beatrice.

TRUDY: *see* Gertrude.

TSIPORA: *see* Zipporah.

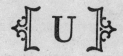

UDELE: (Anglo-Saxon) "woman of great wealth."

ULA: (Celtic) "sea jewel."

ULLAH: (Hebrew) "a burden."

ULRICA: (Teutonic) "ruler of all." Feminine of Ulric. Var. and dim., Ulrika; Rica.

UNA: (Latin) "all truth is one." Var., Ona, Oona.

UNDINE: (Latin) "of water." Var., Ondine.

URANIA: (Greek) "heavenly." Var., Uranie.

URIA: (Hebrew) "light of the Lord." Var., Uriah.

URSULA: (Latin) "she-bear." Var. and dim., Ursa, Ursel, Ursulette, Ursi.

UTA: *see* Ottilie.

VALDA: (Teutonic) "battle heroine." Dim., Val.

VALENTINA: (Latin) "the vigorous and strong." Feminine of Valentine. Var. and dim., Valencia, Valentia, Valerie, Valeria, Valora; Val, Vallie.

VALERIE: *see* Valentina.

VANESSA: (Greek) "the butterfly." Dim., Van, Vanni.

VANIA: (Hebrew) "God's gracious gift." A feminine form of John. Dim., Van.

VASHTI: (Hebrew) "fairest; most lovely woman." Var., Vashta, Vasti.

VEDA: (Sanskrit) "wise."

VELDA: (Teutonic) "of great wisdom." Var., Valeda.

VELMA: *see* Wilhelmina.

VERA: (Latin) "true."

VERDA: (Latin) "young and fresh." Dim., Verdie.

VERN: *see* Laverne.

VERNA: (Latin) "spring-born." Feminine of Vernon. Var., Vernice, Vernita.

VERONICA: (Latin) "true image." Var., Ronnie, Ronny.

VESTA: (Latin) "guardian of the sacred fire," or "vestal virgin." Dim., Esta.

VICKI, VICKY: *see* Victoria.

VICTORIA: (Latin) "the victorious." Feminine of Victor. Var. and dim., Victorie, Victorine; Vicki, Vicky.

VINNA: (Anglo-Saxon) "of the vine." Var., Vina, Vine.

VIOLA: *see* Violet.

VIOLET: (Latin) "modest; shy." Var. and dim., Viola, Violetta, Violette; Vi.

VIONA: *see* Fionna.

VIRGINIA: (Latin) "maidenly; pure." Var. and dim., Virgilia, Virginie; Ginger, Ginny, Jinny, Virg, Virgy.

VITA: (Latin) "life."

VIVIAN: (Latin) "lively; full of life." Var. and dim., Viviane, Vivien, Vivienne; Vi, Viv, Vivi, Vivia, Vivie.

❦[W]❧

WALLIS: (Teutonic) "girl of Wales." Dim., Walli, Wallie, Wally.

WANDA: (Teutonic) "the wanderer." Var., Wenda.

WENDY: *see* Gwendolen.

WENONA: (American Indian) "the first born." Var. and dim., Wenonah, Winona; Winnie, Winny.

WILDA: (Anglo-Saxon) "the untamed; the wild one."

WILFREDA: (Teutonic) "firm peacemaker." Feminine of Wilfred. Dim., Freda.

WILHELMINA: (Teutonic) "protectress." Var. and dim., Velma, Wilma; Mina.

WILLA: (Anglo-Saxon) "desirable." Feminine of William.

WINIFRED: (Teutonic) "friend of peace." Dim., Winnie, Winny.

WINNIE, WINNY: *see* Edwina, Wenona, Winifred.

WINONA: *see* Wenona.

WYNNE: (Celtic) "the fair" or "the white." Var., Wyne.

❦[X]❧

XANTHE: (Greek) "blonde."

XENA: (Greek) "hospitable." Var., Xenia, Zenia.

XINA: *see* Christine.

XYLIA: (Greek) "of the wood."

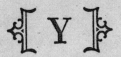

YASMINE: *see* Jasmine.
YETTA: (Teutonic) "mistress of the house."
YOLANDE: (Latin) "modest; shy." Var., Yolanda.
YVETTE: *see* Yvonne.
YVONNE: (French) "the archer." Var. and dim., Ivonne, Yvette, Von, Vonnie.

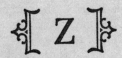

ZABRINA: (Anglo-Saxon) "of the nobility." Var. and dim., Zabrine; Brina.
ZANDRA: (Greek) "friend" or "helper of mankind."
ZEBADA: (Hebrew) "gift of the Lord." Feminine of Zebadiah. Dim., Zeba.
ZELDA: *see* Griselda.
ZENA: (Greek) "hospitable." Var., Zeena, Zenia.
ZENOBIA: (Greek) "having life from Jupiter."
ZERLINA: (Teutonic) "serene and beautiful." Var. and dim., Zerline; Zerla.
ZINAH: (Hebrew) "abundance." Var., Zina.
ZIPPORAH: (Hebrew) "bird." Var. and dim., Ceporah, Tsiporah, Zippora; Tippi, Tippie.
ZOE: (Greek) "life."
ZORA: (Latin) "dawn." Var., Zorah, Zorana, Zorina.
ZULEIKA: (Arabic) "fair."

⁌[NAMES FOR]⁍

Boys

The name that heads the winning slate,
Presidential campaign of 2008
The one that goes to Washington—
May be the name you name your son!

⟦ A ⟧

AARON: (Hebrew) "light; high mountain." Var., Aron.

ABBOT: (Hebrew) "father." Var., Abbott.

ABE, ABIE: *see* Abraham.

ABEL: (Hebrew) "breath."

ABELARD: (Teutonic) "resolute; ambitious."

ABNER: (Hebrew) "of light; bright." Dim., Ab, Abbie.

ABRAHAM: (Hebrew) "father of many; exalted father." Var. and dim., Abram, Avram; Abe, Abie, Bram.

ABRAM: *see* Abraham.

ABSALOM: (Hebrew) "father of peace."

ADAIR: (Celtic) "from the oak-tree ford."

ADALARD, ADELARD: *see* Albert.

ADALBERT: *see* Albert.

ADAM: (Hebrew) "red earth; man of earth." Var. and dim., Adams, Adamson; Ad, Addy.

ADDISON: (Anglo-Saxon) "Adam's descendant."

ADIN: (Hebrew) "voluptuous; sensual." Var., Adan.

ADLAI: (Hebrew) "just."

ADOLPH: (Teutonic) "noble wolf." Var. and dim., Adolf, Adolphe, Adolphus; Dolph.

ADONIS: (Greek) "handsome."

ADRIAN: (Latin) "man of the seacoast." Var., Adrien, Hadrian.

AHAB: (Hebrew) "uncle."

AHERN: (Celtic) "horse lord."

AINSLEY: (Old English) "of a nearby meadow."

ALAN: (Celtic) "harmony." Var., Alain, Allan, Allen.

ALARIC: (Teutonic) "ruler of all." Var. and dim., Alarick, Ulric, Ulrich, Ulrick; Rich, Richie, Rick, Ricky.

ALASTAIR: see Alexander.

ALBAN: (Latin) "white." Var., Alben, Albin, Alva.

ALBERT: (Teutonic) "noble and bright." Var. and dim., Adalard, Adalbert, Adelard, Albrecht, Delbert, Elbert, Ethelbert; Al, Bert, Bertie.

ALBION: see Aubin.

ALCOTT: (Celtic) "from the stone cottage." Var., Alcot.

ALDEN: (Anglo-Saxon) "old friend." Var. and dim., Aldin, Aldwin, Alwin; Al.

ALDO: (Teutonic) "rich."

ALDOUS: (Teutonic) "old; wise." Var., Aldis, Aldus.

ALDRICH: (Teutonic) "king."

ALDWIN: see Alden.

ALEC, ALEX: see Alexander.

ALEXANDER: (Greek) "protector of men." Var. and dim., Alastair, Allister, Sanders, Sandor, Saunders; Al, Alec, Aleck, Alex, Alexis, Alick, Lex, Sandy.

ALEXIS: see Alexander.

ALFONSO: see Alphonse.

ALFRED: (Anglo-Saxon) "wise as an elf." Dim., Al, Alf, Alfie, Alfy.

ALGER: (Anglo-Saxon) "spearman." Var., Algar.

ALGERNON: (French) "with whiskers." Dim., Al, Algie.

ALLISTER: see Alexander.

ALONZO: see Alphonse.

ALOYSIUS: see Lewis.

ALPHONSE: (Teutonic) "prepared for battle." Var. and dim., Alfonso, Alonzo, Alphonso; Lon, Lonny.

ALSTON: (Anglo-Saxon) "from the old manor" or "village."

ALVA: see Alban.

ALVIN: (Teutonic) "friend of all." Var., Alvan, Alwin, Alwyn, Elvin.

AMBERT: (Teutonic) "shining light; bright."

AMBROSE: (Greek) "belonging to the immortals."

AMORY: (Latin) "lover; loving." Var., Amary, Amery.

ANASTATIUS: (Greek) "one who is reborn." Var., Anastas, Anastasius.

ANATOLE: (Greek) "of the East." Var., Anatol.

ANDRE: *see* Andrew.

ANDREW: (Greek) "manly." Var. and dim., Anders, Andreas, Andre, Andrien, Andy.

ANGELO: (Greek) "saintly."

ANGUS: (Celtic) "exceptional; outstanding." Dim., Gus.

ANSELM: (Teutonic) "divine helmet of God." Var., Ansel.

ANSON: (Anglo-Saxon) "the son of Ann."

ANTHONY: (Latin) "of inestimable worth." Var. and dim., Antoine, Anton, Antoni, Antonio, Antony; Tony.

ANTON, ANTONIO: *see* Anthony.

ARCHIBALD: (Teutonic) "truly bold." Var. and dim., Archer; Arch, Archie, Archy.

ARCHIE, ARCHY: *see* Archibald.

ARDEN: (Latin) "fervent; eager and sincere."

ARGUS: (Greek) "watchful; vigilant." Dim., Gus.

ARLIE: *see* Harley.

ARMAND, ARMIN, ARMOND: *see* Herman.

ARMSTRONG: (Old English) "with a strong arm."

ARNOLD: (Teutonic) "strong as an eagle." Dim., Arne, Arnie, Arno.

ARTHUR: (Celtic) "strong as a rock." Var. and dim., Aurthur, Arturo; Art, Artie.

ARTURO: *see* Arthur.

ARVIN: (Teutonic) "a friend of the people." Dim., Arv, Arvie, Arvy.

ASA: (Hebrew) "healer."

ASHER: (Hebrew) "fortunate."

ASHLEY: (Anglo-Saxon) "a dweller in the ash-tree meadow." Dim., Lee.

AUBREY: (Teutonic) "elf-ruler." Dim., Bree, Brey.

AUBIN: (Latin) "fair; white." Var., Albion.

AUGUST: (Latin) "exalted." Var. and dim., Augustin, Augustine, Augustus, Austen, Austin, Gustin; Augie, Gus.

AURICK: see Warrick.

AUSTEN, AUSTIN: see August.

AVERILL: (Anglo-Saxon) "boarlike," or "of April." Var. and dim., Averil, Averill; Av.

AVERY: (Anglo-Saxon) "ruler of the elves."

AVRAM: see Abraham.

AXEL: (Hebrew) "man of peace." Var., Aksel.

AYLMER: see Elmer.

B

BAILEY: (Teutonic) "able."

BAIRD: (Celtic) "the minstrel." Var., Bard.

BALDWIN: (Teutonic) "bold, noble friend."

BANCROFT: (Anglo-Saxon) "from the bean field."

BARCLAY: see Berkeley.

BARD: see Baird.

BARDO: see Bartholomew.

BARNABY: (Hebrew) "son of consolation." Var. and dim., Barnabas; Barney.

BARNARD, BARNET, BARNETT: see Bernard.

BARNEY: see Barnaby, Baruch, Bernard.

BARON: (Teutonic) "of noble blood." Var., Barron.

BARRET: (Teutonic) "mighty as a bear." Var., Barrett.

BARRY: (Celtic) "spear."

BART, BARTH: *see* Barton, Bartholomew.

BARTON: (Anglo-Saxon) "farmer." Dim., Bart, Barth.

BARTHOLOMEW: (Hebrew) "son of the furrows; a ploughman." Var. and dim., Bardo, Barth, Barthol, Bartholemew, Bartholemy, Bartlett, Bartley; Bart, Bat.

BARUCH: (Hebrew) "blessed." Dim., Barney, Barrie, Barry.

BASIL: (Greek) "kingly."

BARTLETT: *see* Bartholomew.

BARTRAM: *see* Bertram.

BAXTER: (Teutonic) "the baker." Dim., Bac.

BAYARD: (French) "of the fiery hair."

BAYNARD: *see* Bernard.

BEN, BENNY: *see* Benedict, Benjamin, Benton.

BENEDICT: (Latin) "blessed." Var. and dim., Benedic, Benedick, Benedix, Bennet, Bennett; Ben, Benny, Dixon.

BENJAMIN: (Hebrew) "son of my right hand." Var. and dim., Benson; Ben, Benjie, Benjy, Bennie, Benny.

BENNETT: *see* Benedict.

BENSON: *see* Benjamin.

BENTON: (Anglo-Saxon) "of the moors." Dim., Ben.

BERKELEY: (Anglo-Saxon) "from the birch meadow." Var., Barclay, Berkley.

BERNARD: (Teutonic) "grim bear." Var. and dim., Barnard, Barnet, Barnett, Baynard, Bernarr, Bernhard; Barney, Bern, Bernie.

BERNHARD: *see* Bernard.

BERT: *see* Albert, Bertram, Burton, Egbert, Herbert.

BERTON: *see* Burton.

BERTRAM: (Latin) "bright raven." Var. and dim., Bartram, Bertrand; Bert.

BERTRAND: *see* Bertram.

BEVAN: (Celtic) "son of Evan." Var., Bevin.

BEVERLEY: (Anglo-Saxon) "from the beaver meadow."

BILL: *see* William.

✓ **BLAIR:** (Celtic) "a place."

BOB: *see* Robert.

BOOTH: (Teutonic) "from a market," or "homelover."

BORDEN: (Old English) "he lives near the boar's den." Var., Barden.

BORIS: (Slavic) "a fighter."

BOWEN: (Celtic) "the son" or "descendant of Owen."

BOYD: (Celtic) "light-haired."

BRAD: dim. of Bradford, Bradley, but also used as an independent name.

BRADFORD: (Anglo-Saxon) "from the broad ford." Dim., Brad, Ford.

BRADLEY: (Anglo-Saxon) "from the broad meadow." Dim., Brad.

BRAM: *see* Abraham, Bramwell.

BRAMWELL: (Old English) "of Abraham's well." Dim., Bram.

BRANDON: *see* Brendan.

BRANT: (Teutonic) "fiery."

BRENDAN: (Celtic) "from the fiery hill." Var., Brandon, Brendon, Brennan.

✓ **BRETT:** (French) "a native of Brittany." Var., Bret.

BRIAN: (Celtic) "strong; powerful." Var., Bryan, Bryant.

✓ **BRICE:** (Celtic) "ambitious; alert." Var., Bryce.

BRIGHAM: (Anglo-Saxon) "a dweller by the bridge."

BROCK: (Celtic) "badger."

BRODERICK: *see* Roderick.

BROMLEY: (Old English) "a dweller in the meadow." Var. and dim., Bromlea, Bromleigh; Brom.

BRUCE: (French) "from the brushwood thicket."

BRUNO: (Teutonic) "brown."

BUDD: (Gaelic) "winner." Var. and dim., Bud; Buddy.

BURKE: (Teutonic) "from the stronghold" or "castle."

BURGESS: (Teutonic) "a townsman." Var. and dim., Bergess, Berger; Berg, Burg.

BURT: *see* Burton.

BURTON: (Anglo-Saxon) "of bright fame." Var. and dim., Berton; Bert, Burt.

BYRON: (French) "from the cottage," or "the bear."

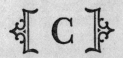

CADMAN: (Celtic) "brave warrior."

CAESAR: (Latin) "born with long hair; leader."

CAL: *see* Caleb, Calvin.

CALDER: (Celtic) "from the river of stones."

CALEB: (Hebrew) "bold; impetuous." Dim., Cal.

CALVERT: *see* Calvin.

CALVIN: (Latin) "bald." Var. and dim., Calvert; Cal.

CAMERON: (Celtic) "bent nose." Dim., Cam, Camm.

CAMPBELL: (French) "from a bright field." Var., Campball.

CAREW: (Celtic) "from this fortress." Dim., Carr.

CAREY, CARY: *see* Charles.

CARL, CARLO, CARLOS, CARROL: *see* Charles.

CARLISLE: (Latin) "from a walled city; island."

CARSON: (Welsh) "his father lives near marshes."

CARTER: (Anglo-Saxon) "cartmaker."

CARVER: (Anglo-Saxon) "one who carves."

CASIMIR: (Slavic) "proclamation of peace." Var. and dim., Casper, Kazimir; Cass, Cassie, Cassy.

CASPAR, CASS, CASSIE: *see* Casimir, Jasper.

CECIL: (Latin) "blind."

CEDRIC: (Celtic) "chieftain."

CHADWICK: (Celtic) "defender." Dim., Chad.

CHALMER: (Teutonic) "king of the household."

CHANCELOR: *see* Chauncey.

CHANDLER: (French) "candlemaker." Dim., Chan.

CHANNING: (Anglo-Saxon) "a regent; knowing."

CHAPIN: (French) "a man of God." Var., Chaplin, Chapland, Chapen.

CHARLES: (Teutonic) "man." Var. and dim., Carey, Carl, Carol, Carrol, Karl, Karol; Charley, Charlie, Chas, Carlo, Carlos, Cary, Chuck.

CHARLTON: (Anglo-Saxon) "of Charles' farm." Var., Carleton, Carlton, Charleton.

CHAUNCEY: (French) "official record-keeper." Var., Chancelor, Chancellor.

CHESTER: (Latin) "of the fortified camp." Var. and dim., Cheston; Chet.

CHET: *see* Chester.

CHILTON: (Anglo-Saxon) "from the farm by the spring." Var., Chelton.

CHRISTIAN: (Latin) "a Christian." Var. and dim., Kristian, Kristin; Chris, Kit.

CHRISTOPHER: (Greek) "Christ-bearer." Dim., Chris, Christie, Christy, Kester, Kit, Kris, Kriss.

CHUCK: *see* Charles.

CLARENCE: (Anglo-Saxon) "bright; illustrious." Dim., Clair, Clare.

CLARK: (Latin) "scholarly; wise." Var., Clarke.

CLAUD: (Latin) "lame." Var. and dim., Claude; Claudy.

CLAUS: *see* Nicholas.

CLAY: *see* Clayton.

CLAYTON: (Anglo-Saxon) "mortal man." Var. and dim., Clayborn, Clayborne; Clay.

CLEM: *see* Clement.

CLEMENT: (Latin) "mild; kind; merciful." Var. and dim., Clemence; Clem.

CLEVE: *see* Clive.

CLIFFORD: (Anglo-Saxon) "from the ford near the cliff." Dim., Cliff.

CLIFTON: (Anglo-Saxon) "from the farm at the cliff."

CLINTON: (Anglo-Saxon) "from the headland farm."

CLIVE: (Anglo-Saxon) "cliff." Var., Cleve.

CLOVIS: *see* Lewis.

CLYDE: (Celtic) "heard from a distance."

COLBY: (Old English) "from the dark farm."

COLE: *see* Coleman, Colin.

COLEMAN: (Celtic) "dove-keeper." Var. and dim., Colman; Col, Cole.

COLIN: (Celtic) "strong; young and virile." Dim., Cole. *See also* Nicholas.

COLLEY: *see* Nicholas.

CONAL: (Celtic) "high and mighty." Var. and dim., Conall, Conan, Conant, Connel, Kynan, Quinn; Con, Conn.

CONANT: *see* Conal.

CONRAD: (Teutonic) "brave counsel." Var. and dim., Konrad; Con, Connie, Curt.

CONROY: (Celtic) "wise."

CONSTANTINE: (Latin) "unwavering; firm." Var. and dim., Constant; Conn.

CONWAY: (Celtic) "a man of the great plains."

CORBIN: (Latin) "the raven." Var. and dim., Corwin; Corby.

CORDELL: (French) "binding cord" or "rope."

COREY: (Celtic) "ravine dweller." Var., Cory.

CORNELIUS: (Latin) "battle horn." Dim., Cornel, Cornell, Neal, Neil.

CORT: *see* Courtenay.

CORWIN: *see* Corbin.

COSMO: (Greek) "universe," or "in good order."

COURTENAY: (French) "a place." Var. and dim., Courtland, Courtney, Court; Cort, Cortie, Corty.

CRAIG: (Celtic) "of the crag" or "stony hill."

CRANDALL: (Old English) "of the valley of the cranes; caretaker of the cranes."

CRAWFORD: (Old English) "of the crow's crossing."

CRISPIN: (Latin) "curly-haired." Var., Crispen.

CROSBY: (Anglo-Saxon) "near the crossroad."

CULBERT: (Teutonic) "noted and bright." Var., Colbert, Cuthbert.

CULVER: (Anglo-Saxon) "gentle; peaceful; dove."

CURRAN: (origin uncertain) "heroic; resolute."

CURT: *see* Conrad, Curtis.

CURTIS: (French) "courteous." Dim., Curt, Kurt.

CUTHBERT: *see* Culbert.

CUTLER: (Old English) "the knife-maker."

CYRIL: (Greek) "Lord."

CYRUS: (Persian) "throne." Dim., Cy, Russ.

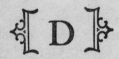

DALE: (Teutonic) "valley dweller." Var., Dalton.

DALLAS: (Celtic) "skilled," or "spirited." Dim., Dal.

DAMON: (Greek) "tame; domesticated." Var., Damian.

DANA: (Scandinavian) "a Dane." Var., Dane.

DANIEL: (Hebrew) "the Lord is judge." Var. and dim., Daniell, Darnell; Dan, Danny.

DANTE: *see* Durand.

DARCY: (French) "from the stronghold." Var., D'Arcy.

DARIUS: (Persian) "a man of many possessions." Var. and dim., Darian, Derian; Darren.

DARRELL: (Anglo-Saxon) "beloved." Var. and dim., Darryl; Darren.

DARREN: dim. of Darius, Darrell, Dorian, etc., but also used as an independent name.

DAVID: (Hebrew) "beloved." Var. and dim., Davis;

Dave, Davie, Davy, Dewey.

DAVIN: (Scandinavian) "the bright man; bright Finn."

DEAN: (Anglo-Saxon) "valley." Var., Deane.

DEARBORN: (Anglo - Saxon) "beloved baby" or "child."

DELBERT: *see* Albert.

DELMAR: (Latin) "of the sea." Var., Delmer.

DEMETRIUS: (Greek) "lover of the earth." Var. and dim., Dimitri, Dmitri; Demmy.

DEMPSTER: (Old English) "a judge; wise." Var. and dim., Dempstor; Dempsey.

DENBY: (Scandinavian) "from the Danish settlement; loyal Dane." Var., Danby.

DENNIS: (Greek) "lover of fine wines." Var. and dim., Denis, Dennison, Denys, Denzil, Dion; Dennie, Denny, Deny.

DENNISON: *see* Dennis.

DEREK, DERRICK, DERK: *see* Theodoric.

DERMOT: *see* Kermit.

DESMOND: (Celtic) "worldly; sophisticated." Dim., Desi.

✓ **DEVIN:** (Celtic) "a poet."

DEWEY: *see* David.

DEXTER: (Latin) "right-handed; dexterous."

DICK: *see* Richard.

DIXON: *see* Benedict.

DILLON: (Celtic) "faithful."

DION: *see* Dennis.

DOANE: (Celtic) "dweller of the sand dune."

DOLPH: *see* Adolph.

DOMINIC: (Latin) "the Lord's." Var. and dim., Dominick; Dom, Dominy, Nic, Nick, Nicky.

DONALD: (Celtic) "ruler of the world." Var. and dim., Donal, Donall, Donnell; Don, Donn, Donnie, Donny.

DORAN: (Greek) "the stranger." Var., Dorran.

DORIAN: (Greek) "from the town of Dori." Dim.,

Darren, Dore, Dorey, Dory. *See also* Isidore.

DOUGLAS: (Celtic) "from the black stream." Dim., Doug.

DOYLE: (Celtic) "the dark stranger; newcomer."

DREW: (Teutonic) "skilled; honest." Var., Dru, Drue.

DRISCOLL: (Celtic) "the speaker or interpreter."

DRUCE: (Celtic) "wise man; capable and adept."

DUANE: (Celtic) "singing." Var., Dwane, Dwayne.

DUDLEY: (Anglo-Saxon) "a place." Dim., Dud, Lee.

DUKE: (Latin) "leader."

DUNCAN: (Celtic) "warrior of dark skin." Dim., Dunc.

DUNSTAN: (Anglo-Saxon) "from the brown stone hill."

DUNTON: (Old English) "of the farm over the hill."

DURAND: (Latin) "enduring." Var., Dante, Durant.

DURWARD: (Anglo-Saxon) "the doorkeeper." Var., Durware, Durwood, Derwood.

DURWIN: (Anglo-Saxon) "dear friend." Var. Durwyn.

DUSTIN: (Teutonic) "strong-hearted leader."

DWAYNE: *see* Duane.

DWIGHT: (Teutonic) "light."

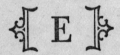

EARL: (Anglo-Saxon) "nobleman; chief." Var., Earle, Early, Erle, Errol.

EATON: (Anglo-Saxon) "of the river" or "riverside."

EBEN: (Hebrew) "stone."

EBENEZER: (Hebrew) "stone of help." Dim., Eb.

EBERHART: *see* Everard.

EDAN: (Celtic) "flame."

EDGAR: (Anglo-Saxon) "lucky spear; fortunate warrior." Dim., Ed, Eddie.

EDLIN: *see* Edwin.

EDMUND: (Anglo-Saxon) "fortunate" or "rich protector." Var. and dim., Edmond; Ed, Eddie, Ned, Neddy.

EDRIC: (Anglo-Saxon) "rich ruler." Var., Edrick.

EDSEL: (Anglo-Saxon) "profound; deep thinker."

EDSON: (Anglo-Saxon) "the son of Ed." Var., Edison.

EDWARD: (Anglo-Saxon) "prosperous guardian." Var. and dim., Eduard; Ed, Eddie, Eddy, Ned, Neddy, Ted, Teddy.

EDWIN: (Anglo-Saxon) "wealthy friend." Var. and dim., Edlin; Ed, Eddie, Eddy.

EFREM: *see* Ephraim.

EGAN: (Teutonic) "formidable." Var., Egon.

EGBERT: (Anglo-Saxon) "bright and shining sword." Dim., Bert, Bertie.

ELBERT: *see* Albert.

ELDON: (Teutonic) "respected; older." Var. and dim., Elden, Eldon; El.

ELDRIDGE: (Anglo-Saxon) "wise advisor." Var., Eldred, Eldrid.

ELDWIN: (Anglo-Saxon) "wise friend; advisor." Var., Eldwen.

ELEAZAR: (Hebrew) "helped by God." Var., Eliezer, Lazarus, Lazar.

ELEPH: (Hebrew) "strong as an ox."

ELI: (Hebrew) "the highest." Var., Elia, Ely.

ELIAS: (Hebrew) "the Lord is God." Var., Elihu, Elijah, Eliot, Elliott, Ellis.

ELLARD: (Teutonic) "nobly brave."

ELLIOT, ELLIS: *see* Elias.

ELLERY: (Teutonic) "of the alder trees." Var., Elery.

ELLISON: (Hebrew) "son of Elias." Var., Elison.

ELLSWORTH: (Anglo-Saxon) "lover of the earth; farmer." Var., Elsworth.

ELMER: (Anglo-Saxon) "noble; famous." Var., Aylmer.

ELMO: (Greek) "friendly."

ELROY: (Latin) "royal." Var. and dim., Leroy; Roy.

ELTON: (Anglo-Saxon) "from the old farm" or "village."

ELVIN: *see* Alvin.

ELWIN: (Anglo-Saxon) "a friend to elves." Var. and dim., Elwyn; Winn, Wynn.

EMERSON: (Old English) "a son of Emory."

EMIL: (Teutonic) "industrious." Var., Emlyn.

EMMANUEL: (Hebrew) "God is with us." Var. and dim., Immanuel, Manuel; Manny.

EMMET: (Anglo-Saxon) "ant; industrious." Var. and dim., Emmett; Em, Emmy.

EMORY: (Teutonic) "work-leader; ambitious." Var., Emery, Merrick.

ENOCH: (Hebrew) "devoted."

ENOS: (Hebrew) "mortal."

ENRICO: *see* Henry.

EPHRAIM: (Hebrew) "abounding in fruitfulness." Var. and dim., Efrem; Eph.

ERASMUS: (Greek) "kindly."

ERIC: (Teutonic) "kingly." Var. and dim., Erich, Erick, Erik; Rick, Ricky.

ERLAND: (Teutonic) "noble eagle."

ERLE: *see* Earl.

ERNEST: (Teutonic) "sincere; intent." Dim., Ern, Ernie.

ERROL: *see* Earl.

ERSKINE: (Celtic) of uncertain meaning.

ERWIN: *see* Irvin.

ESMOND: (Anglo-Saxon) "gracious protector."

ESTES: (Latin) "from a famous ruling house."

ETHAN: (Hebrew) "steadfast."

ETHELBERT: *see* Albert.

EUGENE: (Greek) "noble; well-born." Dim., Gene.

EUSTACE: (Greek) "fruitful."

EVAN: *see* John.

EVELYN: (Old English) "a dear youth."

EVERARD: (Teutonic) "mighty as a boar." Var. and dim., Eberhart, Everett; Ev.

EVERETT: *see* Everard.

EWALD: (Latin) "the bearer of good news."

EZEKIEL: (Hebrew) "God's strength." Dim., Zeke.

EZRA: (Hebrew) "the helpful" or "helper." Dim., Ez.

FABIAN: (Latin) "prosperous farmer." Dim., Fabe.

FAIRFAX: (Anglo-Saxon) "fair" or "yellow-haired."

FAIRLEY: (Anglo-Saxon) "from the far meadow." Var. and dim., Fairlie, Farley; Farl.

FALKNER: (Anglo-Saxon) "falcon hunter" or "trainer." Var., Faulkner, Fowler.

FARAND: (Teutonic) "attractive; pleasant." Var. and dim., Farrand, Farant; Ran.

FARLEY: *see* Fairley.

FARRELL: (Celtic) "the valorous one." Var., Farrel.

FAULKNER: *see* Falkner.

FAVIAN: (Latin) "a man of understanding."

FAXON: (Teutonic) "renown for his hair."

FELIX: (Latin) "fortunate."

FENTON: (Anglo-Saxon) "dweller of the marshland."

FERDINAND: (Teutonic) "bold venture." Var. and dim., Fernand, Fernando, Hernando; Ferd, Ferde, Ferdie.

FERGUS: (Celtic) "best choice," or "strong man."

FERNAND, FERNANDO: *see* Ferdinand.

FERRIS: (Celtic) "rock."

FIRMAN: (Anglo-Saxon) "traveler to distant places."

FISK: (Scandinavian) "the fisherman." Var., Fiske.

FITZGERALD: (Teutonic) "a son of Gerald."

FITZPATRICK: (Teutonic) "a son of Patrick."

FLAVIAN: (Latin) "fair" or "blond." Var., Flavius.

FLETCHER: (French) "arrow-maker." Dim., Fletch.

FLEMING: (Anglo-Saxon) "the Dutchman." Dim., Flem.

FLORIAN (Latin) "flowering; blooming." Dim., Flory.

FLOYD: *see* Lloyd.

FORD: *see* Bradford.

FORREST: (Teutonic) "from the woods." Var., Forest.

FOSTER: (Teutonic) "forester; keeper of the preserve."

FOWLER: *see* Falkner.

FRANCIS: (Teutonic) "free." Var. and dim., Frank, Franchot, Franz; Frankie, Fran.

FRANK: *see* Francis.

FRANKLIN: (Teutonic) "a free man." Dim., Frank.

FRANZ: *see* Francis.

FREEMAN: (Anglo-Saxon) "one born free." Var., Freemon.

FREDERICK: (Teutonic) "peaceful chieftain." Var. and dim., Frederic, Fredric; Fred, Freddie, Freddy, Fritz.

FRITZ: *see* Frederick.

FULTON: (Anglo-Saxon) "from a field" or "farm town."

G

GABRIEL: (Hebrew) "God is mighty." Dim., Gabby, Gabe.

GADMAN: (Hebrew) "the fortunate." Var., Gadmon.

GALE: (Celtic) "lively."

GALEN: (Greek) "healer."

GALVIN: (Celtic) "the sparrow." Dim., Vin, Vinny.

GAMALIEL: (Hebrew) "the Lord is my recompense."

GAR: Dim. of any name beginning with "Gar"; used also as an independent name.

GARDINER: (Teutonic) "flower lover." Var., Gardner.

GARETT: (Anglo-Saxon) "mighty spear." Var. and dim., Gareth, Garreth, Garrett, Garth, Gerard, Jaret; Garry, Gary, Gerry, Jary.

GARIBALD: (Old English) "a welcome addition."

GARNER: (Teutonic) "the defender; noble guardian."

GARNET: (Latin) "grain; red jewel." Var., Garnett.

GARRICK: (Teutonic) "mighty warrior." Dim., Rick.

GARTH: (Anglo-Saxon) "yard-keeper."

GARVIN: (Teutonic) "battle friend." Dim., Gar, Gary.

GARY: see Garett, Garvin.

GASPAR: see Jasper.

GASTON: (Teutonic) "from Gascony."

GAVIN: see Gawain.

GAWAIN: (Teutonic) "battle hawk." Var., Gavin.

GAYLORD: (Anglo-Saxon) "the joyous nobleman."

GEBER: (Hebrew) "strong."

GENE: see Eugene.

GEOFFREY: (Teutonic) "God's peace; peace of the land." Var. and dim., Godfrey, Jeffers, Jeffery, Jeffrey, Jeffry; Geof, Geoff, Jeff.

GEORGE: (Greek) "farmer; tiller of the soil." Var. and dim., Gustaf, Gustavus; Gus, Gussie. See also August.

GERALD: (Teutonic) "mighty spearman." Var. and dim., Garold, Gereld, Gerrald, Jereld, Jerold, Jerrold; Gerry, Gery, Jer, Jerry.

GERARD: see Garett.

GERRY: see Garett, Gerald.

GERVASE: (Teutonic) "spear vassal," or "honorable." Var. and dim., Gervais, Jarvis, Jervis; Jarv, Jarvey.

GIAN: see John.

GIDEON: (Hebrew) "brave warrior; indomitable spirit."

GIFFORD: (Teutonic) "gift."

GILBERT: (Teutonic) "bright pledge." Var. and dim., Gilpin, Wilbert, Wilbur; Gil.

GILES: (Latin) "shield bearer." Var. and dim., Gile, Gilles; Gil, Gilly.

GILROY: (Latin) "the king's faithful servant."

GIOVANNI: *see* John.

GLADWIN: *see* Goodwin.

GLEN: (Celtic) "from the valley." Var., Glenn, Glynn.

GODDARD: (Teutonic) "of a firm nature." Var., Godderd, Goddord.

GODFREY: *see* Geoffrey.

GOODMAN: (Teutonic) "good man."

GOODWIN: (Teutonic) "good and faithful friend." Var., Gladwin, Godwin.

GORDON: (Anglo-Saxon) "from the cornered hill."

GRAHAM: (Teutonic) "from the gray home." Var. and dim., Graeme; Ham.

GRANT: (French) "great."

GRANVILLE: (French) "of the big town."

GRAYSON: (Old English) "a judge's son." Var. and dim., Greyson; Gray, Grey.

GREGORY: (Greek) "vigilant." Dim., Greg.

GRESHAM: (Anglo-Saxon) "from the grazing land."

GRIFFITH: (Celtic) "red-haired." Var. and dim., Griffin, Rufus; Griff, Rufe.

GRISWOLD: (Teutonic) "from the wild gray forest."

GROVER: (Anglo-Saxon) "grove-dweller."

GUNTHER: (Teutonic) "bold warrior." Var., Gunar, Guntar, Gunter, Gunthar.

GUS: *see* Angus, August, Gustave.

GUSTAVE: (Scandinavian) "noble staff." Var. and dim., Gustaf, Gustavus; Gus, Gussie. *See also* August.

GUSTIN: *see* August.

GUTHRIE: (Celtic) "war serpent," or "war hero."

GUY: (French) "guide." Var., Guido, Guyon, Wiatt, Wyatt.

GWYN: (Celtic) "fair."

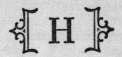

[H]

HADDEN: (Old English) "of the moors." Var., Haden.

HADRIAN: *see* Adrian.

HAINES: (Teutonic) "from a vined cottage." Var., Haynes.

HAL: *see* Harold, Henry.

HALDEN: (Teutonic) "half Dane." Var., Haldane.

HALE: (Old English) "from a sturdy stock."

HALL: (Old English) "from the master's house."

HALSEY: (Anglo-Saxon) "from Hal's island." Var., Halsy.

HAMILTON: (French) "from the mountain hamlet."

HAMISH: *see* James.

HAMLIN: *see* Henry.

HANK: *see* Henry.

HANLEY: (Anglo-Saxon) "of the high meadow." Var., Hanleigh, Henleigh, Henley, Henry.

HANS: *see* John.

HANSEL: (Scandinavian) "a gift from the Lord."

HARCOURT: (French) "from an armed court."

HARDY: (Teutonic) "of hardy stock."

HARIM: (Hebrew) "flat-nosed."

HARLAN: (Teutonic) "from the battle land."

HARLEY: (Anglo-Saxon) "from the hare's" or "stag's meadow." Var. and dim., Harden, Harleigh, Hartley; Arley, Arlie, Harl, Hart.

HAROD: (Hebrew) "the loud terror." Var., Harrod.

HAROLD: (Anglo-Saxon) "army commander." Var. and dim., Harald, Herald, Hereld, Herold, Herrick; Hal, Harry.

73

HARRIS: (Old English) "a son of Henry."

HARRY: *see* Harold, Henry.

HARTLEY: *see* Harley.

HARTWELL: (Teutonic) "from the deer's spring." Var. and dim., Harwell, Harwill; Hart.

HARVEY: (French) "bitter." Var. and dim., Hervey; Harv, Harve, Herv, Herve.

HAYDEN: (Teutonic) "from the hedged hill."

HAYES: (Old English) "from the woods; the hunter."

HEATH: (Anglo-Saxon) "from the vast wasteland."

HECTOR: (Greek) "steady; unswerving." Dim., Heck.

HEINRICK, HENDRICK, HENDRIK: *see* Henry.

HENLEY: *see* Hanley.

HENRY: (Teutonic) "home ruler." Var. and dim., Enrico, Hamlin, Heinrick, Hendrick, Hendrik, Henri; Hal, Hank, Harry, Hen.

HERALD: *see* Harold.

HERBERT: (Teutonic) "bright warrior." Dim., Bert, Bertie, Herb, Herbie.

HERMAN: (Teutonic) "noble warrior." Var. and dim., Armand, Armin, Armond, Armyn, Hermon; Herm, Hermie.

HERNANDO: *see* Ferdinand.

HERROD: (Hebrew) "heroic conqueror." Var., Herod.

HERVEY: *see* Harvey.

HERWIN: (Teutonic) "a friend" or "lover of battle."

HEYWOOD: (Teutonic) "from the dark green forest."

HEZEKIAH: (Hebrew) "God is strength." Var., Hesketh.

HILARY: (Latin) "cheerful; merry." Var., Hilaire, Hillary.

HILLEL: (Hebrew) "greatly praised."

HILLIARD: (Teutonic) "war guardian" or "protector."

HILTON: (Old English) "from the house on the hill."

HIRAM: (Hebrew) "most noble; exalted." Dim., Hy.

HOBART: *see* Hubert.

HOLBROOK: (Anglo-Saxon) "from the valley brook."
HOLDEN: (Teutonic) "kind."
HOLLIS: (Anglo-Saxon) "dweller by the holly trees."
HOMER: (Greek) "pledge."
HORACE: (Latin) "timekeeper." Var. and dim., Horatio, Horatius; Race.
HORATIO: *see* Horace.
HOSEA: (Hebrew) "salvation."
HOUSTON: (Anglo-Saxon) "from a mountain town."
HOWARD: (Teutonic) "chief guardian." Dim., Howie.
HOWLAND: (Old English) "of the hills."
HOYT: *see* Hubert.
HUBERT: (Teutonic) "shining of mind." Var. and dim., Hobart, Hoyt, Hubbard; Hubie.
HUGH: (Teutonic) "mind; intelligence." Var. and dim., Huey, Hughes, Hugo; Hughie.
HUGO: *see* Hugh.
HUMBERT: (Teutonic) "bright home." Dim., Bert, Bertie.
HUME: (Teutonic) "lover of his home."
HUMPHREY: (Teutonic) "a protector of the peace." Var., Humfrey.
HUNTER: (Old English) "the hunter." Var., Huntley.
HYMAN: (Hebrew) "life." Masculine of Eve. Var. and dim., Hymen; Hy, Hymie.

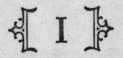

IAN: *see* John.
ICHABOD: (Hebrew) "the glory has departed."
IGNATIUS: (Latin) "the fiery and ardent." Var. and dim., Ignace, Ignatz.
IGOR: (Scandinavian) "hero." Var., Inge, Ingmar.

IMMANUEL: *see* Emmanuel.

INGRAM: (Teutonic) "the raven." Var., Ingraham.

INNESS: (Celtic) "from the island." Var., Innis.

IRA: (Hebrew) "watcher."

IRVIN: (Anglo-Saxon) "sea friend." Var. and dim., Ervin, Ervine, Erwin, Irving, Irwin, Marvin, Mervin, Merwin; Irv, Marv, Merv.

IRVING: *see* Irvin.

IRWIN: *see* Irvin.

ISAAC: (Hebrew) "laughing."

ISIDORE: (Greek) "a gift." Var. and dim., Isador, Isadore, Isidor; Dore, Dorian, Dory, Issy, Iz, Izzy.

ISMAN: (Hebrew) "a loyal husband."

ISRAEL: (Hebrew) "the Lord's warrior" or "soldier." Dim., Issy, Iz, Izzy.

IVAN: *see* John.

IVAR: (Scandinavian) "military archer." Var., Iver, Ives, Ivon, Ivor, Ivo, Yves.

IVES: *see* Yves.

⸢ J ⸣

JABEZ: (Hebrew) "cause of sorrow." Dim., Jabe.

JACK: *see* James, John.

JACOB: *see* James.

JACQUES: *see* James.

JAMES: (Hebrew) "the supplanter." Var. and dim., Hamish, Jacob, Jacques, Seamus, Shamus; Jack, Jake, Jakie, Jamesy, Jamie, Jem, Jemmie, Jemmy, Jim, Jimmie, Jimmy, Jock, Jocko.

JAN: *see* John.

JARED: (Hebrew) "the descending" or "descendant."

JARLATH: (Latin) "man of control."

JARVIS: *see* Gervase.

JASON: (Greek) "healer."

JASPER: (Persian) "treasure-bringer." Var. and dim., Caspar, Gaspar, Kaspar; Cass.

JAVIER: *see* Xavier.

JAY: (Anglo-Saxon) "crow," or "lively." Also used as a dim. for names beginning with the initial J.

JECONIAH: (Hebrew) "gift of the Lord."

JEDEDIAH: (Hebrew) "beloved by the Lord." Var. and dim., Jedidiah; Jed, Jeddy.

JEFFREY: *see* Geoffrey.

JEGAR: (Hebrew) "witness our love." Var., Jeggar, Jegger.

JEREMIAH: *see* Jeremy.

JEREMY: (Hebrew) "exalted by the Lord." Var. and dim., Jeremiah, Jeremias; Jerry.

JERMYN: (Latin) "a German." Var. and dim., Germaine, Jermaine; Gerry, Jer, Jerry.

JEROME: (Greek) "holy." Dim., Jer, Jerry.

JERELD, JEROLD, JERROLD: *see* Gerald.

JERVIS: *see* Gervase.

JESSE: (Hebrew) "God's gift" or "grace." Dim., Jess.

JETHRO: (Hebrew) "outstanding; excellent." Dim., Jeth.

JEVON: *see* John.

JIM: *see* James.

JOAB: (Hebrew) "praise the Lord."

JOACHIM: (Hebrew) "the Lord will judge."

JOB: (Hebrew) "the persecuted; the afflicted."

JOCK: *see* James, John.

JOEL: (Hebrew) "Jehovah is God." Dim., Joe, Joey.

JOHAN, JOHANN: *see* John.

JOHN: (Hebrew) "God's gracious gift." Var. and dim., Evan, Gian, Giovanni, Hans, Ian, Ivan, Jan, Jevon, Johan, Johann, Jon, Juan, Sean, Shane, Shawn, Zane; Jack, Jock, Johnnie, Johnny, Jonnie, Jonny.

JONAH: (Hebrew) "peace."

JONAS: (Hebrew) "dove." Var., Jonah, Jone.

JONATHAN: (Hebrew) "gift of the Lord." Dim., Jon.

√ **JORDAN:** (Hebrew) "descending."

JORGE: *see* George.

JOSEPH: (Hebrew) "He shall add." Var. and dim., José, Joe, Joey, Jos.

JOSES: (Hebrew) "helped by the Lord."

JOSHUA: (Hebrew) "whom God has saved." Dim., Josh.

JOSIAH: (Hebrew) "he is healed by the Lord."

JOTHAM: (Hebrew) "God is perfect." Dim., Joe.

JUAN: *see* John.

JUDD: (Hebrew) "descendant."

JUDSON: (Teutonic) "the son of Judd."

JULES: *see* Julius.

JULIAN: *see* Julius.

JULIUS: (Latin) "divinely youthful." Var. and dim., Joliet, Jules, Julian; Jule, Juley, Julie.

JUNIUS: (Latin) "born in June." Dim., June, Junie.

JURGEN: *see* George.

JUSTIN: (Latin) "the just." Var. and dim., Justus, Just.

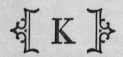

K

KANE: (Celtic) "bright; radiant." Var., Kayne.

KARL: *see* Charles.

KASPAR: *see* Jasper.

KAY: (Latin) "rejoiced in." Also used as a dim. for names beginning with K.

KEITH: (Celtic) "a place."

KELSEY: (Teutonic) "from the water." Var., Kelcey.

KENDALL: (Celtic) "chief of the valley." Var. and dim., Kendal; Ken, Kenny.

KENDRICK: (Anglo-Saxon) "royal ruler." Var. and dim., Kendricks, Kenric; Ken.

KENELM: (Anglo-Saxon) "brave helmet." Dim., Ken.

KENLEY: (Old English) "of the king's meadow." Var., Kenleigh.

KENNETH: (Celtic) "handsome." Var. and dim., Kennet; Ken, Kenny, Kent.

KENT: *see* Kenneth.

KENWAY: (Anglo-Saxon) "the brave soldier." Dim., Ken, Kenny.

KENYON: (Celtic) "fair-haired." Dim., Ken, Kenny.

KERBY: *see* Kirby.

KERMIT: (Celtic) "free." Var. and dim., Dermot; Kerry.

KERR: (Celtic) "dark; mysterious." Var. and dim., Kerrin, Kieran; Kerrie, Kerry.

KESTER: *see* Christopher.

KEVIN: (Celtic) "kind; gentle." Dim., Kev.

KIM: *see* Kimball.

KIMBALL: (Anglo-Saxon) "royally brave." Var. and dim., Kemble, Kimble; Kim.

KING: (Anglo-Saxon) "king."

KINGSLEY: (Anglo-Saxon) "from the king's meadow."

KIRBY: (Teutonic) "from the church village." Var. and dim., Kerby; Kerr.

KIRK: (Scandinavian) "of the church; living close to the church." Var., Kerk.

KIT: *see* Christopher.

KLAUS: *see* Nicholas.

KNUTE: (Danish) "kind."

KONRAD: *see* Conrad.

KURT: *see* Curtis.

KYLE: (Gaelic) "fair and handsome." Var., Kile.

KYNAN: *see* Conal.

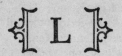

[L]

LABAN: (Hebrew) "white."

LACHLAN: (Celtic) "warlike."

LAIRD: (Celtic) "proprietor."

LAMBERT: (Teutonic) "rich in land." Dim., Bert, Lam.

LAMONT: (Scandinavian) "a lawyer." Var., Lamond.

LANCE: (Anglo-Saxon) "spear." Var. and dim., Lancelot, Launce, Launcelot; Lancey.

LANDON: (Anglo-Saxon) "from the long hill." Var., Langdon, Langston.

LANE: (Anglo-Saxon) "from the country road."

LANG: (Teutonic) "tall."

LANGDON: *see* Landon.

LARS, LARZ: *see* Lawrence.

LATHROP: (Anglo-Saxon) "of the village." Var., Lathrope.

LATIMER: (Anglo-Saxon) "Latin master or teacher."

LAUNCELOT: *see* Lance.

LAUREN, LAURENCE, LAURENT: *see* Lawrence.

LAWRENCE: (Latin) "laurel; crowned with laurel." Var. and dim., Lauren, Laurence, Laurent, Loren, Lorenz, Lorenzo, Lorin; Larry, Lars, Laurie, Lori, Lorry.

LAWTON: (Old English) "man of refinement." Var., Laughton.

LAZARUS: *see* Eleazar.

LEANDER: (Greek) "lion-man; brave." Dim., Lee.

LEAR: (Teutonic) "of the meadow."

LEE: (Anglo-Saxon) "meadow; sheltered." Var., Leigh. Used also as dim. of Leander, Leo, Leopold.

LEICESTER: *see* Lester.

LEIGH: *see* Lee.

LELAND: (Anglo-Saxon) "of the lowlands." Var., Leeland.

LEMUEL: (Hebrew) "consecrated to God." Dim., Lem.

LEO: (Latin) "lion; brave as a lion." Var. and dim., Leon, Leonard, Leonardo, Lion, Lionel, Lyon; Len, Lennie, Lenny.

LEON, LEONARD, LEONARDO: *see* Leo.

LEOPOLD: (Teutonic) "brave for the people; patriotic." Dim., Lee, Leo, Lepp.

LEROY: *see* Elroy.

LES: *see* Leslie, Lester.

LESLIE: (Celtic) "from the gray fort." Var. and dim., Lesley (usually fem.), Les.

LESTER: (Anglo-Saxon) "from the army" or "camp." Var. and dim., Leicester; Les.

LEWIS: (Teutonic) "renowned in battle." Var. and dim., Aloysius, Clovis, Lewes, Louis, Ludovick, Ludvig, Luigi, Luis; Lew, Lou, Louie.

LINCOLN: (Celtic) "from the place by the pool; river bank." Dim., Linc, Link.

LINUS: (Hebrew) "flaxen-haired."

LIONEL: *see* Leo.

LLEWELLYN: (Celtic) "lion-like; lightning."

LLOYD: (Celtic) "gray," or "dark." Var., Floyd.

LON, LONNY: *see* Alphonse.

LOREN, LORENZO, LORRY: *see* Lawrence, Loring.

LORIMER: (Latin) "lover of horses."

LORING: (Teutonic) "coming from Lorraine." Var. and dim., Loredo, Loren, Lorry.

LOT: (Hebrew) "veiled."

LOTHAR: *see* Luther.

LOUIS: *see* Lewis.

LOWELL: (Anglo-Saxon) "beloved." Var., Lovel, Lovell.

LUCAS: *see* Lucius.

LUCIUS: (Latin) "light." Var. and dim., Lucas, Lucian; Luce, Luke, Lukey.

LUDOVICK, LUDVIG: *see* Lewis.

LUIGI: *see* Lewis.

LUKE: *see* Lucius.

LUTHER: (Teutonic) "renowned warrior." Var., Lothair, Lothar, Lothario.

LYLE: (French) "from the island." Var., Lisle.

LYMAN: (Old English) "man of the plains."

LYNDON: (Old English) "of the linden tree."

LYNN: (Anglo-Saxon) "from the waterfalls." Var., Linn.

LYON: *see* Leo.

LYSANDER: (Greek) "liberator." Dim., Sandy.

MAC: (Celtic) "the son of." Dim. for any name beginning with "Mac" or "Mc."

MADDOCK: (Celtic) "fire," or "beneficent." Var., Maddox, Madoc.

MADEN: *see* Matthew.

MADISON: (Teutonic) "mighty in battle."

MALCOLM: (Celtic) "dove."

MALLORY: (Latin) "luckless."

MALVIN: (Celtic) "chief." Var. and dim., Melvin; Mal.

MANUEL: *see* Emmanuel.

MARCO, MARCUS: *see* Mark.

MARK: (Latin) "belonging to Mars; a warrior." Var. and dim., Marc, Marcel, March, Marco, Marcus, Marcy, Marek, Mars, Martin, Martyn; Marty.

MARLEN, MARLIN, MARLON: *see* Merlin.

MARMADUKE: (Celtic) "sea leader." Dim., Duke.

MARSDEN: (Anglo-Saxon) "from the marsh valley." Dim., Denny.

MARSHALL: (French) "marshal." Var. and dim., Marshal; Marsh.

MARTIN: *see* Mark.

MARVIN: *see* Irvin.

MASON: (Latin) "worker in stone."

MATTHEW: (Hebrew) "God's gift." Var. and dim., Maddis, Maden, Mathias, Matthias; Mat, Matt, Matty.

MAURICE: (Latin) "dark; Moorish." Var. and dim., Morel, Morice, Morris, Murray, Seymour; Maurey, Maury, Morry.

MAXIMILIAN: (Latin) "the greatest." Var. and dim., Maxim; Max, Maxey, Maxie.

MAXWELL: (Anglo-Saxon) "he lives near the spring."

MAYNARD: (Anglo-Saxon) "mightily strong."

MEDWIN: (Teutonic) "strong friend." Dim., Winnie.

MELVILLE: (French) "a place." Dim., Mel.

MELVIN: *see* Malvin.

MERCER: (Latin) "merchant."

MEREDITH: (Celtic) "sea protector." Var., Meridith.

MERLE: (Latin) "blackbird." Var., Merl.

MERLIN: (Anglo-Saxon) "hawk; falcon." Var. and dim., Marlen, Marlin, Marlon; Marl, Merl.

MERRICK: *see* Emory.

MERRILL: *see* Myron.

MERTON: (Anglo-Saxon) "from the place by the sea."

MERVIN, MERWIN: *see* Irvin.

MEYER: (Teutonic) "farmer." Var., Mayer.

MICAH: (Hebrew) "like unto the Lord."

MICHAEL: (Hebrew) "Godlike." Var., and dim., Mitchell; Mickey, Mike, Mitch.

MILBURN: (Old English) "of the stream by the mill."

MILES: (Greek) "millstone." Var., Milo, Myles.

MILLARD: (Old English) "a miller."

MILTON: (Anglo-Saxon) "from the mill town." Dim., Milt.

MITCHELL: see Michael.

MONROE: (Celtic) "from the red swamp." Var., Munro.

MONTAGUE: (Latin) "from the pointed mountain." Var. and dim., Montagu; Monte.

MONTE: see Montague, Montgomery.

MONTGOMERY: (French) "mountain hunter." Dim., Monte, Monty.

MORDECAI: (Hebrew) "a wise counselor."

MORGAN: (Celtic) "from the sea," or "sea-white."

MORLEY: (Anglo-Saxon) "from the moor meadow."

MORRIS: see Maurice.

MORTIMER: (Latin) "from the quiet water." Dim., Mort, Mortie, Morty.

MORTON: (Anglo-Saxon) "from the moor village." Dim., Mort, Morty.

MOSES: (Egyptian) "saved from the water." Var. and dim., Mose, Moss; Moe.

MOSS: see Moses.

MUIR: (Celtic) "Moor."

MUNRO: see Monroe.

MURDOCH: (Celtic) "prosperous from the sea." Var., Murdock, Murtagh.

MURRAY: (Celtic) "sailor." Var., Murrey, Murry. See also Maurice.

MYRON: (Greek) "fragrant." Var., Merrill.

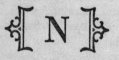

NALDO: (Teutonic) "power."

NARCISSUS: (Greek) "self-loving."

NATHANIEL: (Hebrew) "gift of God." Var. and dim., Nathan, Nathanael; Nat, Nate, Natie, Natty.

NEAL: (Celtic) "champion." Var., Neale, Neil; Nealey. *See also* Cornelius.

NED: *see* Edmund, Edward, Norton.

NELSON: (Celtic) "son of Neal." Var., Neilson. *See also* Cornelius.

NERO: (Italian) "black; dark."

NESTOR: (Greek) "venerable wisdom." Var. and dim., Nessim; Nessie.

NEVILLE: (Latin) "from the new town." Var. and dim., Nevil; Nev.

NEVIN: (Anglo-Saxon) "nephew." Var., Nevins.

NEWEL, NEWELL: *see* Noel.

NEWTON: (Anglo-Saxon) "from the new estate."

NICHOLAS: (Greek) "victory of the people." Var. and dim., Nichol, Nicholl, Nicolas, Niles; Claus, Colin, Colley, Klaus, Nick, Nicky.

NICODEMUS: (Greek) "the people's conqueror." Dim., Nick, Nicky.

NIGEL: (Latin) "dark; black."

NILES: *see* Nicholas.

NOAH: (Hebrew) "rest; comfort; peace."

NOBLE: (Latin) "renowned; noble." Var., Nobel, Nolan.

NOEL: (Latin) "Christmas." Var., Newel, Newell, Noelle.

NOLAN: see Noble.

NOLL: see Oliver.

NORBERT: (Teutonic) "sea brightness." Dim., Bert.

NORMAN: (Teutonic) "man from the north," or "of Normandy." Var. and dim., Normand, Norris; Norm, Normie.

NORRIS: *see* Norman.

NORTON: (Anglo-Saxon) "from the north place." Dim., Ned, Norty.

NORVIN: (Teutonic) "man from the north."

NORWARD: (Teutonic) "the guard at the northern gate." Var., Norword, Norwood.

❧[O]❧

OAKLEY: (Anglo-Saxon) "from the oak-tree meadow."

OBADIAH: (Hebrew) "the Lord's servant." Dim., Obe.

OCTAVIUS: (Latin) "eighth." Var. and dim., Octave, Octavian, Octavus; Tavey.

ODELL: (Teutonic) "wealthy man." Var., Odin, Odo.

ODORIC: (Latin) "son of a good man."

OGDEN: (Anglo-Saxon) "from the oak valley."

OLAF: (Scandinavian) "peace," or "reminder." Var., Olen.

OLIVER: (Latin) "olive; peace." Var. and dim., Olivier; Ollie, Noll, Nollie, Nolly.

OMAR: (Hebrew) "talkative."

ORDWAY: (Anglo-Saxon) "spear-fighter."

OREN: (Hebrew) "pine." Var., Orin, Orrin.

ORION: (Latin) "giant."

ORLANDO: *see* Roland.

ORMOND: (Teutonic) "ship man." Var., Orman, Ormand.

ORSON: (Latin) "bear." Var., Orsini, Orsino.

ORVILLE: (French) "lord of the manor." Var., Orvil.

OSBERT: (Anglo-Saxon) "divinely bright." Dim., Bert, Bertie, Berty, Oz, Ozzie.

OSBORN: (Anglo-Saxon) "divinely strong." Var., Osborne, Osbourne.

OSCAR: (Anglo-Saxon) "divine spear." Dim., Os, Ozzie.

OSGOOD (Teutonic) "gift of our Lord."

OSMOND: (Teutonic) "he is protected by God." Var. and dim., Osmand, Osmund; Ozzie.

OSWALD: (Anglo-Saxon) "divine power." Dim., Os, Oz.

OTIS: (Greek) "keen-eared."

OTTO: (Teutonic) "wealthy; prosperous."

OWEN: (Celtic) "young warrior." Var., Owain.

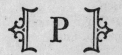

PADDY: *see* Patrick.

PAGE: (French) "servant to the royal court." Var., Paige.

PAINE: (Latin) "countryman; rustic; pagan." Var., Payne.

PALEY: *see* Paul.

PALMER: (Latin) "the palm-bearer," or "pilgrim."

PARK: (Anglo-Saxon) "of the park." Var., Parke.

PARNELL: *see* Peter.

PARRY: (French) "guardian; warder; protector."

PATRICK: (Latin) "noble; patrician." Var. and dim., Padraic, Patric, Peyton; Paddy, Pat, Patsy, Patty, Rick.

PAUL: (Latin) "little." Var. and dim., Paley; Paulie.

PAXTON: (Teutonic) "from afar; a traveler." Var., Packston, Paxon.

PAYNE: *see* Paine.

PEARCE, PIERCE: *see* Peter.

PEDRO: *see* Peter.

PEMBROKE: (Celtic) "from the headland."

PERCIVAL: (French) "valley-piercer." Var. and dim., Perceval, Purcell; Perce, Percy.

PERCY: *see* Percival.

PEREGRINE: (Latin) "wanderer." Dim., Perry.

PERRY: (Anglo-Saxon) "pear tree." Dim., Perr.

PETER: (Greek) "rock; stone." Var. and dim., Parnell, Pearce, Pedro, Pernell, Perrin, Petrie, Pierce, Pierre, Pietro; Pete, Petey, Petie.

PEYTON: *see* Patrick.

PHELAN: (Celtic) "wolf; brave as a wolf."

PHILBERT: (Teutonic) "a radiant soul." Var. and dim., Filbert; Bert.

PHILIP: (Greek) "lover of horses." Var. and dim., Phelps, Phillip; Flip, Phil.

PHILO: (Greek) "love."

PHINEAS: (Hebrew) "oracle; mouth of brass."

PIERRE: *see* Peter.

PIERSON: (Greek) "son of Peter." Var. and dim., Pearson, Peerson, Pierce.

PIUS: (Latin) "pious."

PORTER: (Latin) "doorkeeper," or "gatekeeper."

POWELL: (Celtic) "alert."

PRENTICE: (Latin) "learner; apprentice." Var., Prentiss.

PRESCOTT: (Anglo-Saxon) "of the priest's house."

PRESTON: (Anglo-Saxon) "of the priest's place."

PRINCE: (Latin) "prince."

PRIOR: (Latin) "superior; head of a monastery." Var., Pryor.

PROCTOR: (Latin) "leader." Var., Procter.

PUTNAM: (Anglo-Saxon) "dweller of the pond."

Q

QUARTUS: (Latin) "fourth son."

QUENTIN: (Latin) "fifth." Var. and dim., Quintin; Quent, Quint.

QUILLON: (Latin) "sword." Dim., Quill.
QUINBY: (Scandinavian) "of the womb of woman."
QUINCY: (Latin) "from the fifth son's place."
QUINN: *see* Conal.

[R]

RADBURN: (Old English) "he lives by the red brook." Var., Radbourne, Radburne.
RADCLIFFE: (Anglo-Saxon) "from the red cliff."
RADFORD: (Old English) "he lives by the red valley." Var., Radferd, Radley.
RALEIGH: (Old English) "of the deer field."
RALPH: *see* Randolph.
RALSTON: (Old English) "of the house of Ralph." Var., Ralfston, Rolfston.
RAMON: *see* Raymond.
RAMSEY: (Teutonic) "from the ram's island."
RANDALL: *see* Randolph.
RANDOLPH: (Anglo-Saxon) "protected; advised by wolves." Var. and dim., Ralph, Randal, Randall, Rolf, Rolfe, Rolph; Randy, Rand.
RAPHAEL: (Hebrew) "healed by God." Var. and dim., Rafael, Raffaello; Raff.
RAYBURN: (Old English) "of the deer's brook."
RAYMOND: (Teutonic) "wise protection." Var. and dim., Ramon, Raymund; Ray.
READE: (Anglo-Saxon) "red-haired." Var., Reed, Reid.
REDMOND: (Teutonic) "adviser; protector."
REGAN: (Celtic) "royal; king."
REGINALD: (Teutonic) "mighty ruler." Var. and dim., Raynold, Reinhold, Reynold, Rinaldo, Ronald; Reg, Reggie, Ron, Ronnie, Ronny.

REID: *see* Reade.

REINHOLD: *see* Reginald.

REMUS: (Latin) "oarsman."

REUBEN: (Hebrew) "behold a son!" Var. and dim., Ruben; Rube, Ruby.

REX: (Latin) "king."

RICHARD: (Teutonic) "wealthy and powerful." Var. and dim., Ricardo; Dick, Dicky, Rick, Ricky, Ritch, Ritchie.

RICHMOND: (Teutonic) "powerful protector."

RICK: a dim. of Alaric, Elric, Richard, etc., but used also as an independent name.

RIDGLEY: (Old English) "he lives by the meadow's edge."

RINALLDO: *see* Reginald.

ROBERT: (Teutonic) "of bright, shining fame." Var. and dim., Roberto, Robin, Rupert; Bob, Bobbie, Bobby, Rab, Rob, Robbie, Robby.

ROBIN: *see* Robert.

RODERICK: (Teutonic) "renowned ruler." Var. and dim., Broderick, Roderic, Rodrick; Rod, Roddy, Rory.

RODMANN: (Teutonic) "redhead." Var. and dim., Rodman, Rod, Roddy.

RODNEY: (Teutonic) "renowned." Dim., Rod, Roddie, Rodi, Roddy.

ROGER: (Teutonic) "renowned spearman; famous warrior."

ROLAND: (Teutonic) "fame of the land." Var. and dim., Orlando, Rollin, Rowland; Rollo, Roley.

ROLLO: *see* Roland, Rudolph.

ROLPH: *see* Randolph.

ROMEO: (Latin) "pilgrim to Rome."

ROMULUS: (Latin) "citizen of Rome."

RONALD: *see* Reginald.

RORY: (Celtic) "ruddy; red-haired." Var., Rorie, Rorry.

ROSCOE: (Teutonic) "from the deer forest." Dim., Ros, Roz.

ROSS: (Teutonic) "horse."

ROSWELL: (Teutonic) "mighty steed." Dim., Ros, Roz.

ROY: (Latin) "king."

ROYCE: (French) "son of the king."

RUBE, RUBY: *see* Reuben.

RUDOLPH: (Teutonic) "famed wolf." Var. and dim., Rollin, Rudolf; Dolph, Rolfe, Rollo, Rolph, Rudy.

RUFUS: (Latin) "red-haired." Var. and dim., Griffin, Griffith; Griff, Rufe.

RUPERT: *see* Robert.

RUSS: *see* Cyrus, Russell.

RUSSELL: (Anglo-Saxon) "like a fox." Var. and dim., Russel; Russ.

RUTHERFORD: (Old English) "from the cattle ford." Var., Rutherfurd.

SALISBURY: (Old English) "from the guarded palace."

SALVADOR: (Latin) "of the Savior." Dim., Sal.

SAMSON: (Hebrew) "sunlike." Var. and dim., Sampson, Simpson, Simson; Sam, Sammy, Sim.

SAMUEL: (Hebrew) "name of God." Dim., Sam, Sammy.

SANBORN: (Old English) "of the sandy beach." Var. and dim., Sanburn, Sanborne; Sandy.

SANDERS: (Greek) "son of Alexander." Var., Saunders. *See also* Alexander.

SANDY: *see* Alexander, Sanford.

SANFORD: (Old English) "by the sandy crossing." Var. and dim., Sandford; Sandy.

SARGENT: (Latin) "a military attendant."

SAUL: (Hebrew) "longed for; desired."

SAWYER: (Celtic) "man of the woods."

SAXON: (Teutonic) "from a Saxon town." Var., Saxen.

SCHUYLER: (Dutch) "a scholar; a wise man."

✓ **SCOTT:** (Latin) "a Scotsman." Dim., Scot, Scottie, Scotty.

SEAMUS: *see* James.

✓ **SEAN, SHAWN:** *see* John.

SEBASTIAN: (Greek) "respected; reverenced."

SEDGEWICK: (Old English) "from the village of victory." Var., Sedgewinn.

SELBY: (Teutonic) "from the manor farm." Var., Shelby.

SELIG: *see* Zelig.

SELWYN: (Teutonic) "friend at the manor."

SERLE: (Teutonic) "bearing arms" or "weapons."

SETH: (Hebrew) "chosen."

SETON: (Anglo-Saxon) "from the place by the sea."

SEWARD: (Anglo-Saxon) "defender of the coast."

SEWELL: (Teutonic) "victorious on the sea." Var., Sewel.

SEYMOUR: (French) "follower of St. Maur." *See also* Maurice.

✓ **SHANE:** *see* John.

SHAW: (Anglo-Saxon) "from the grove."

SHELBY: *see* Selby.

SHELDON: (Anglo-Saxon) "from the hill-ledge" or "shelly valley." Var. and dim., Shelton; Shel, Shell, Shelly.

SHELLEY: (Anglo-Saxon) "from the ledge" or "shelly meadow." Dim., Shel, Shell.

SHEPARD: (Anglo-Saxon) "sheep-tender." Var. and

dim., Shepherd, Sheppard; Shep, Shepp.

SHEPLEY: (Anglo-Saxon) "of the sheep meadow." Var. and dim., Sheply; Shep.

SHERARD: (Anglo-Saxon) "a brave soldier." Var., Sherrard.

SHERIDAN: (Celtic) "wild man; savage." Dim., Sherry.

SHERLOCK: (Old English) "a short-haired son."

SHERMAN: (Anglo-Saxon) "wool-shearer; sheepcutter." Dim., Sherm.

SHERWIN: (Anglo-Saxon) "a true friend."

SHERWOOD: (Anglo-Saxon) "bright forest."

SIDNEY: (French) "a follower of St. Denis." Var. and dim., Sydney; Sid, Syd.

SIGFRID: (Teutonic) "glorious peace." Var., Siegfried.

SIGMUND: (Teutonic) "victorious protector."

SILAS: (Latin) "of the forest." Var. and dim., Silvan, Silvanus, Silvester, Sylvan, Sylvester; Si.

SIMON: (Hebrew) "heard." Var., Simeon.

SIMPSON, SIMSON: *see* Samson.

SINCLAIR: (Latin) "saintly; shining light."

SION: (Hebrew) "exalted."

SLOAN: (Celtic) "warrior."

SOL: (Latin) "sun." Used also as dim. of Solomon.

SOLOMON: (Hebrew) "peaceable; wise." Dim., Sol, Solly.

SPENCER: (French) "storekeeper; dispenser of provisions." Var. and dim., Spenser; Spence.

SPRAGUE: (Old English) "the quick one." Var., Sprage.

STACY: (Latin) "stable companion." Var., Stacey.

STAFFORD: (Old English) "of the landing place." Var., Staffard, Staford.

STANFORD: (Anglo-Saxon) "of the stony crossing."

STANHOPE: (Old English) "from the stony vale."

STANLEY: (Slavonic) "pride of the camp." Var. and

dim., Stanleigh; Stan, Lee.

STANTON: (Anglo-Saxon) "from the stony place."

STEFAN: *see* Stephen.

STEPHEN: (Greek) "crown; garland." Var. and dim., Stefan, Steffen, Steven; Steve, Stevie.

STERLING: (Teutonic) "good value; honest; genuine." Var., Stirling.

STEVEN: *see* Stephen.

STEWART: (Anglo-Saxon) "keeper of the estate." Var. and dim., Steward, Stuart; Stew, Stu.

STILLMAN: (Anglo-Saxon) "quiet; gentle."

STODDARD: (Anglo-Saxon) "keeper of horses."

STUART: *see* Stewart.

SUMNER: (Latin) "one who summons and calls."

SUTTON: (Anglo-Saxon) "from the south town" or "village."

SYDNEY: *see* Sidney.

SWAINE: (Teutonic) "boy." Var., Swane, Swain.

SYLVESTER: *see* Silas.

T

TAD, THAD: *see* Theodore, Thaddeus.

TALBOTT: (Anglo-Saxon) "bloodhound." Var., Tallbot, Talbot.

TAM, TAMMANY, TOMAS: *see* Thomas.

TATE: (Teutonic) "cheerful." Var., Tait, Taite.

TAVIS: (Celtic) "son of David."

TAYLOR: (Latin) "the tailor."

TED, TEDDY: *see* Edward, Theodore, Theodoric.

TERENCE: (Latin) "tender." Var. and dim., Terrence, Torrance; Torin, Terry.

TERRILL: (Teutonic) "belonging to Thor; martial."

TERRY: *see* Terence.

THADDEUS: (Hebrew) "praise to God." Dim., Tad, Thad.

THATCHER: (Anglo-Saxon) "a mender of roofs." Var., Thacher, Thackeray, Thaxter.

THAYER: (Teutonic) "of the nation's army."

THEOBALD: see Tybalt.

THEODORE: (Greek) "gift of God." Var. and dim., Feodor, Feodore, Tudor; Dore, Tad, Ted, Teddie, Teddy, Theo.

THEODORIC: (Teutonic) "the people's ruler." Var. and dim., Derek, Derrick, Tedric; Derk, Ted, Teddie, Teddy.

THOMAS: (Hebrew) "the twin." Var. and dim., Tammany, Tomas; Tam, Tammy, Thom, Tom, Tommy.

THOR: (Scandinavian) "the thunderous one."

THORNTON: (Anglo-Saxon) "from the thorny place."

THORPE: (Anglo-Saxon) "from the small village."

THURLOW: (Old English) "of Thor's mountain." Var., Thorlow.

THURMAN: (Scandinavian) "under Thor's protection." Var., Thorman.

THURSTON: (Scandinavian) "Thor's jewel" or "stone."

TILDEN: (Anglo-Saxon) "from a fertile valley."

TIMOTHY: (Greek) "honoring God." Dim., Tim, Timmie.

TITUS: (Latin) "safe; saved."

TOBIAS: (Hebrew) "God's goodness." Var. and dim., Tobit; Tobe, Toby.

TODD: (Latin) "the fox."

TOM, TOMAS, TOMMY: see Thomas.

TONY: see Anthony.

TORRANCE, TORIN: see Terence.

TOWNSEND: (Anglo-Saxon) "from the end of town."

TRACEY: (Anglo-Saxon) "the brave defender." Var., Tracy.

TRAVERS: (Latin) "from the crossroad." Var., Travis.

TRENT: (Latin) "swift."

TREVOR: (Celtic) "careful traveler."

TRISTAN: (Latin) "sorrowful."

TRUMAN: (Anglo-Saxon) "a faithful man."

TURNER: (Latin) "worker with the lathe."

TY: a dim. for any name beginning with "Ty."

TYBALT: (Teutonic) "leader of the people." Var. and dim., Theobald, Thibaut, Tybald; Ty.

TYLER: (Anglo-Saxon) "maker of tiles" or "bricks." Dim., Ty.

TYRONE: (Celtic) of uncertain meaning. Dim., Ty.

TYSON: (Teutonic) "son of the German." Dim., Sonny, Ty.

[U]

ULRIC, ULRICH: *see* Alaric.

ULYSSES: (Greek) "angry one; wrathful."

UNNI: (Hebrew) "modest."

UPTON: (Anglo-Saxon) "from the hill town."

URBAN: (Latin) "from the city; urbane; sophisticated."

URIAH: (Hebrew) "the Lord is my light." Var., Urias, Uriel.

UZIEL: (Hebrew) "a mighty force." Var., Uzziel.

[V]

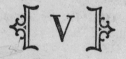

VACHEL: (French) "keeper of the cattle." Var., Vachil.

VAIL: (Anglo-Saxon) "from the valley." Var., Vale, Valle.

VAL: (Teutonic) "might; power." Also dim. of any name beginning with "Val."

VALENTINE: (Latin) "healthy; strong; valorous." Var., Valente, Valiant.

VALERIAN: (Latin) "strong; belonging to Valentine."

VANCE: (Dutch) "the son of a famous family." Var., Van.

VARIAN: (Latin) "clever; capricious."

VAUGHAN: (Celtic) "the small." Var., Vaughn.

VERE: (Latin) "true; faithful."

VERNON: (Latin) "growing green; flourishing." Var., Vern, Verne.

VICTOR: (Latin) "the conqueror." Var. and dim., Victoir, Vittorio; Vic, Vick.

VIGOR: (Latin) "vigor."

VINCENT: (Latin) "the conqueror." Dim., Vin, Vince.

VINSON: (Anglo-Saxon) "son of Vinn," thus, "the conqueror's son."

VIRGIL: (Latin) "strong; flourishing." Var. and dim., Vergil; Virg, Virgie, Virgy.

VITO: (Latin) "vital."

VIVIEN: (Latin) "lively."

VLADIMIR: (Slavonic) "the ruler of all." Var., Vladamir, Waldemar, Wladimir.

VOLNEY: (Teutonic) "most popular." Var., Volny.

WADE: (Anglo-Saxon) "mover; wanderer."

WADSWORTH: (Old English) "from Wade's castle."

WALCOTT: (Anglo-Saxon) "cottage dweller."

97

WALDEMAR: (Teutonic) "strong; famous." Var. and dim., Waldimar; Waldo.

WALKER: (Anglo-Saxon) "forest walker."

WALLACE: (Teutonic) "a foreigner." Var. and dim., Wallis, Walsh; Wallie, Wally.

WALSH: *see* Wallace.

WALTER: (Teutonic) "powerful; mighty warrior." Var. and dim., Walters; Wallie, Wally, Walt.

WARD: (Anglo-Saxon) "watchman; guardian."

WARE: (Anglo-Saxon) "always careful."

WARING: (Anglo-Saxon) "the cautious soul."

WARNER: (Teutonic) "protecting warrior."

WARREN: (Teutonic) "game warden."

WARRICK: (Teutonic) "strong ruler." Var., Aurick, Vareck, Varick.

WATSON: (Anglo-Saxon) "warrior's son."

WAYLAND: (Teutonic) "from the land near the highway."

WAYNE: (Teutonic) "wagonmaker." Var., Waine, Wain.

WEBSTER: (Anglo-Saxon) "weaver." Dim., Web, Webb.

WELBY: (Scandinavian) "from the farm by the spring."

WELDON: (Teutonic) "from a hill near the well."

WENDELL: (Teutonic) "wanderer." Var., Wendel.

WESCOTT: (Teutonic) "dwells at west cottage." Dim., Wes.

WESLEY: (Anglo-Saxon) "from the west meadow." Var. and dim., Wellesley; Wes.

WHITELAW: (Anglo-Saxon) "of the white hill."

WHITNEY: (Anglo-Saxon) "from a white island."

WILBERT, WILBUR: *see* Gilbert.

WILFRED: (Teutonic) "firm peacemaker." Var. and dim., Wilfrid; Fred, Freddie.

WILL, WILLY: *see* William.

WILLIAM: (Teutonic) "determined protector." Var. and dim., Wilhelm, Willet, Willis; Bill, Billie, Billy, Will, Willy.

WILSON: (Teutonic) "son of William." Dim., Wil.

WINFIELD: (Anglo-Saxon) "from the friendly field."

WINIFRED: (Teutonic) "friend of peace." Var. and dim., Winfred, Winfrid; Fred, Win.

WINSLOW: (Teutonic) "from the friendly hill." Dim., Win.

WINSTON: (Anglo-Saxon) "from the friendly town." Var. and dim., Winton; Win.

WINTHROP: (Teutonic) "from the friendly village."

WOLFE: (Teutonic) "a wolf."

WOLFRAM: (Teutonic) "respected; feared."

WLADIMIR: see Vladimir.

WOODLEY: (Anglo-Saxon) "from the wooded meadow."

WOODROW: (Anglo-Saxon) "from the hedgerow in the wood." Dim., Woodie.

WORD: *see* Ward.

WRIGHT: (Anglo-Saxon) "craftsman; worker."

WYATT: (French) "a guide."

WYLIE: (Anglo-Saxon) "beguiling; charming."

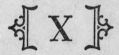

X

XAVIER: (Arabic) "bright." Var., Javier.

XENOS: (Greek) "stronger."

XERXES: (Persian) "king."

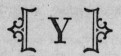

Y

YALE: (Teutonic) "payer; yielder."
YANCY: (French) "Englishman." Var., Yancey.
YATES: (Anglo-Saxon) "the gate dweller" or "protector."
YORK: (Latin) "sacred tree." Var., Yorick, Yorke.
YVES: (Scandinavian) "an archer." Var., Ives, Yvon.

Z

ZACHARIAH: (Hebrew) "the Lord's remembrance." Var. and dim., Zacharias, Zachary; Zach, Zack.
ZACHARY: *see* Zachariah.
ZANE: *see* John.
ZEBADIAH: (Hebrew) "the Lord's gift." Var. and dim., Zebedee; Zebe, Zeb.
ZEBULON: (Hebrew) "dwelling place." Dim., Lonny, Zeb.
ZEKE: *see* Ezekiel.
ZELIG: (Teutonic) "blessed." Var., Selig.
ZENAS: (Greek) "Jupiter's gift."
ZEPHANIAH: (Hebrew) "hidden by the Lord." Dim., Zeph.

YOUR BABY'S
HOROSCOPE

A guide to his (or her) personality traits;
traditional birthstones; traditional flowers;
traditional colors.

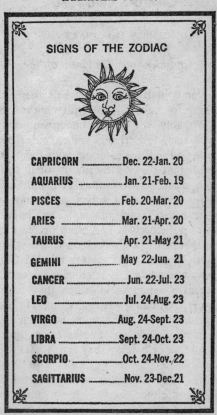

SIGNS OF THE ZODIAC

CAPRICORN	Dec. 22-Jan. 20
AQUARIUS	Jan. 21-Feb. 19
PISCES	Feb. 20-Mar. 20
ARIES	Mar. 21-Apr. 20
TAURUS	Apr. 21-May 21
GEMINI	May 22-Jun. 21
CANCER	Jun. 22-Jul. 23
LEO	Jul. 24-Aug. 23
VIRGO	Aug. 24-Sept. 23
LIBRA	Sept. 24-Oct. 23
SCORPIO	Oct. 24-Nov. 22
SAGITTARIUS	Nov. 23-Dec. 21

BABIES BORN UNDER THE SIGN OF

Capricorn

The Most Conscientious Children of the Zodiac

Perhaps you will be annoyed when these children are not willing to make friends with children of their own age. Probably you won't understand why they prefer to pick their few friends among older boys and girls. Perhaps you will try to argue with them about it, with the result that they "withdraw in their shell" and become even more self-conscious and solitary. Don't scold them for being shy or sullen, as it may seem to you. They are never "good mixers." They have mental resources within themselves and often prefer their own company to that of other children, especially those who seem "babyish" to the more mature-minded Capricorn children. Why not guide this intelligence constructively by giving them some tasks at which they may be of service to you? They can be depended upon to discharge any task given them with more thoroughness and patience than most children. They are not the ones to quit in the middle of a task; they finish whatever they begin.

You need not worry about how they will get along in their school work either, for they are inclined to study hard and put into practical use the knowledge that they gain. Not infrequently, you will find them interested in some line of study leading to a trade or a profession. They will be ambitious to get to the top of the field and have the patience to build their success on a firm foundation of lessons well learned. Don't, however, expect them to be hail-fellows-well-met. Never will they aspire to be cheer leaders of the football team. If they have anything to do with the team, it will probably be as business managers, not star players.

Saturn's influence as ruler of Capricorn bestows the valuable qualities of efficiency, levelheadedness, and conscientiousness to these children; but it also fosters a tendency toward pessimism unless direct effort is made to prevent such development. You can be very helpful in teaching them to find the brighter side of life rather than to dwell on the darker side. Diligence, stability, and practicality are key words assigned to the children born under Capricorn. This does not indicate, however, that they crave only responsibilities and duties in their lives. There is the natural enjoyment of fun in their makeup which needs to be brought out for an airing every so often. See that there is time set aside regularly for recreational indulgences in order that they may develop a well-rounded personality.

Capricorn—with its ruler, Saturn—has dominion over the bones, outer layer of the skin, joints, and the hardening processes of the body. These children must guard against disorders which can result from their tendency to become despondent. You must teach them to transcend this untoward potential by seeing to it that they have a warm, comfortable, and congenial home; nourishing food; and sufficient physical exercise to keep their minds in healthy functioning condition at all times.

BABIES BORN UNDER THE SIGN OF

Aquarius

(JANUARY 21–FEBRUARY 19)

The Most Loyal Children of the Zodiac

These children do not enjoy solitude. Companionships are important to them, however young or old they may be. As their parent, you will be wise to make chums or companions of them rather than assume the role of stern master, for these children, on the whole, do not need strict discipline and are more obedient to your wishes than children of most of the other signs. You may be sure that they will ask more than the usual number of questions, for they will want to know the reason that they should not play with matches or put a negative and positive electric wire together, but once you have explained to them that matches can cause fires or phosphorus poisoning and that positive and negative currents blow out fuses when they meet, you will find them willing to forego the experiments they would otherwise make.

In their search for companionship, they will prefer to be with those who are older than they are. Their intelligence will be above the average child of their age, and since they are agreeable companions, the chief danger is that they will be spoiled with too much attention and allowed too many privileges for their years.

One of the best means of development for these children is through caring for pets. You can give them great happiness by bringing home a stray kitten or a puppy. Pets which require outdoor care or exercise will also serve to take these childen out of doors more than they would be otherwise, for their natural tendency is to prefer indoor activities or reading. They are naturally ambitious to learn and to open to themselves the avenues of culture and recognition to which education is the gate. Their ambition is more to "be someone" than to accumulate material possessions, and education is, to them, a means to this end.

Since Aquarius is the sign which rules the bloodstream, infections caused by diseased tonsils or bad teeth are not infrequently the cause of illness in children of this sign. Aquarius also rules the ankles; sprained ankles are a frequent accident. But you won't have to bandage many broken knuckles or doctor many black eyes, for they aren't the ones to look for fights or participate in them if they can avoid it. Their nature is, on the whole, inclined toward shyness, and they are more disposed to yield to the opinion of others if doing so secures harmony. Their friendships, when formed, are likely to be lasting, since they will never be the first to break up an existing condition. This fixed and constant nature also results in a certain amount of stubbornness, and you will find them easier to control by affection than by force. In planning their education, philosophy, science, and literature are lines in which they will take the greatest interest. There is frequently inventive ability along scientific lines, and they will also find great interest in humanitarian work. These children rarely lead what would be called a dull life, and this is shared naturally by family and friends.

BABIES BORN UNDER THE SIGN OF

Pisces

(FEBRUARY 20–MARCH 20)

The Most Imaginative Children of the Zodiac

If you are given to mottos, the best one you can tack up for the Pisces children is that about bad companions corrupting good morals, for they are more susceptible to the influence of their playmates, for good or evil. The reason for this is that Pisces is a negative sign, extremely sensitive to any influence around it and with less than the usual power to resist these influences. It is, therefore, up to you to see that they do not come under unfavorable influences until they are old enough to be able to know right from wrong.

Their easygoing, self-indulgent nature makes them exceedingly fond of rich foods—and with a strong tendency to drink. These disastrous tendencies have more chance to be indulged because these children are agreeable, sympathetic, kind, and friendly, and, therefore, much sought after as companions. Unless they are taught self-control along these lines, they may not only ruin their lives but ruin their health as well.

If a restraining and constructive influence is brought to bear upon them, however, you will find them developing into idealistic, amiable, imaginative, and orderly young persons. They are capable of acquiring a good education; and because of their agreeable disposition, they will cause little trouble to their teachers. They are not ones to seek fights—in fact, they are so inclined to peaceful measures that they will often allow others to impose upon them rather than start fights.

You may trust them to keep secrets, for in spite of their talkativeness, they are dependable and honest and seldom betray any trusts reposed in them. Their lack of physical energy, however, will make them averse to hard work, and they may shrink from household chores assigned to them, but if you insist upon this work, you will find that they do it in an effortless and methodical way—probably in order to make it as easy for themselves as possible. Training in distasteful tasks during the early years will be excellent discipline for them. Don't think it unusual if they spend hours in daydreaming; Neptune, their ruling planet, is irresponsible, mystic, and romantic, and his children show all of these qualities. Because of their sensitive nature, they will be confused and hurt by a reprimand rather than resentful, and they may feel very sorry for themselves when you punish them. The things they fail to do rather than those they do will be your chief cause for complaint against them. You will find them forgetful, careless about picking up after themselves, neglectful of their possessions, and not very attentive to your instructions —usually because they are daydreaming of something a thousand miles away. Don't be lacking in understanding and sympathy for them; on the other hand, don't coddle them or fight their battles for them—their greatest need is to develop will power and self-confidence in order to be prepared to face life and its problems. They need a sturdy anchor early in life lest they become mental wanderers.

BABIES BORN UNDER THE SIGN OF

Aries

(MARCH 21–APRIL 20)

The Most Brilliant Children of the Zodiac

As prospective parents of Aries children, you may become prematurely gray worrying about what hair-raising stunt they will try next, whether their last bump will subside before they raise another and whether any head can be injured as many times as theirs and still function properly. In Aries children, you will have a bundle of Mars (their ruler) energy, enthusiasm, and dynamic power ready to explode at any—or without any—provocation. Their vitality is so abundant that they just must be doing something all the time, and usually it is something which requires physical expression.

They are born leaders—and born fighters, and if they do not play at fighting, they fight at playing! They are venturesome to the extent of foolhardiness, and when an idea occurs to them—as it does with more than the usual frequency of childish ideas—they never stop to figure out the consequences of their action.

Aside from the physical restraint which they need, they must be taught moderation in personal conduct, in speech, and in their personal outlook upon life. They are never "shrinking violets" and self-assertion, rather than self-consciousness, is their chief characteristic.

The energy and enthusiasm of Aries children may make them hard workers and able to earn money, but they will be very poor savers. They are not very good at sticking to a task once their enthusiasm has worn off. The qualities of leadership are manifested in their relations with their playmates, for Aries children can get more work out of them than they would ever do of their own accord. This very power of leadership makes Aries children a great force for either good or evil, and if their energy is misdirected, they can become gang leaders instead of leaders for the cause of justice and order. It is essential that this powerful nature be directed from childhood into the right paths.

The emotional nature of Aries children is ardent, demonstrative, and frequently idealistic. They are happy to feel themselves the champions of the weaker and less fortunate. Cultivate in them this sense of responsibility for others, and, above everything else, try to teach them to stick to one job until they have finished it, and not to scatter their enthusiasm over a multitude of projects.

The nature of Mars and the mental qualities of Aries are manifested in these children's hasty speech, quick temper, enthusiasm, quick wit, and love of freedom. They are the pioneers in the new undertakings, and they will find their greatest success in executive positions where their aggressiveness and superabundant energy will have the fullest scope possible.

In matters of health, aside from accidents caused by the recklessness and daring which are so typical, there is danger of fevers, headaches, and kidney ailments. For these children, adequate rest and relaxation are requisites for maintenance of health, for they are inclined to use up vitality faster than they can generate it.

BABIES BORN UNDER THE SIGN OF

Taurus

(APRIL 21–MAY 21)

The Most Popular Children of the Zodiac

You will find that Taurus children are never carried away by wild enthusiasms, nor will they dash away to follow any leader who would be accepted by less stable and strong-willed children. They resemble the patient bull, who must be annoyed and tormented before aroused to anger. But, as you may know, once a bull decides to fight, he makes a thorough and complete job of it. Taurus children do the same.

Unless Taurus children are actually tormented until their patient nature can endure no more, however, they will be reluctant to fight—partly because they are naturally slow to act and partly because they abhor pain—and fights usually result in a missing tooth or two. Their nature is fundamentally gentle, and you may, with proper handling, manage them for years without seeing any evidence of anger or temper. You will never forget it, though, if their temper is aroused, for under these conditions, they are not only furious and headstrong, but stubborn in yielding to the opinion or authority of others. But on the whole, they will give you far less to worry about than most other children.

Their natural secretiveness adds to their reserved nature, but their practical and constructive qualities offset the less friendly characteristics. Music, art, literature, and all the beauty of nature will appeal to them. In speech or writing, however, they may be somewhat inarticulate. They feel strongly, but express themselves with difficulty. The practical and conservative side of their nature will show itself in their love of home and birthplace. In their friendships, they are both faithful and warm-hearted. They are, however, much more easily hurt than one would believe from their self-sufficient and somewhat too confident manner. Unless they are praised, loved, and encouraged, they tend to become indifferent and will underrate their own abilities. Praise them, but don't indulge them. Don't let them take life too easy, for this indifference could develop into actual laziness. Keep a keen eye on their natural inclination to overeat, especially since this fondness for good things tends to lead in later life to congestion of the kidneys, enlargement of the liver, heart disease, and rheumatism—all results of overindulgence of the appetite. Conditions affecting the throat are specially marked in those born under Taurus.

Their mind is steady, unimaginative, slow in action but extremely fixed when that action has finally developed. In brief, they are the perfect example of the conservative virtues—"slow but sure" and "haste makes waste." Their appreciation of the material blessings of this world will tend to make them strive to accumulate the means to purchase comfort and pleasure—two things which they consider most important in their scheme of life. Sometimes they secure these comforts and pleasures as rewards of their own thrift, sometimes as a legacy; in any case, their material lot in life is more fortunate than average.

BABIES BORN UNDER THE SIGN OF

Gemini

(MAY 22–JUNE 21)

The Most Alert Children of the Zodiac

Only the parents of twins can appreciate the problem that falls to the parents of Gemini children. For Gemini is the sign of the twins, and Gemini children will frequently represent such a "split personality" that they do not understand even their own nature or know what they actually want from life. One of the best things you can do for them is to teach them, when young, to stick to one line, instead of trying to carry on two or more interests.

These children are inclined to lack concentration and to "talk your ear off." They are the ones who are told that "children should be seen and not heard"—probably because they make themselves heard more than any other member of the family. But you should realize that they possess a high-strung, highly organized nervous system. Unnecessary talk, in either children or adults, is a sign of overtaxed nerves, as well as strain on the nerves of those who must listen.

Part of the constant questioning of these children is due to an actual desire for information, for they are always quick-witted and bright, but their curiosity is rather superficial. They want to know something about everything that happens to cross their path, but they will not persist in one line of thought long enough to learn much on any subject or stick to one task or one line of work long enough to make an outstanding success of it. They have a quick, active, and curious mind, and they will constantly look for change. Because they are adaptable, they do not hesitate to try new roads. Your problem will be to keep them on the old road long enough to "get somewhere."

Another point to keep in mind in understanding these children is that their bodies need stimulation much more than their minds do. Let them do the active physical things which will give an outlet for their nervous energy, but keep them mentally calm. Do not, unless you want children with "nerves" that will prove a real detriment in later years, tell them bedtime stories of Bluebeard or Jack the Giant Killer, for their over-wrought imagination will work even in sleep, and you will be awakened by their terrified "nightmares," in which the giant is pursuing them. Put them to bed early, for they need sleep, and let nothing in their minds disturb their rest, for they need all they can get. Even afternoon naps are excellent to quiet their nerves—and probably yours, too!

In spite of their highly organized nervous system, and general lack of robustness, they will seldom suffer from serious illness with the exception of lung trouble, a disease to which they are especially subject, since Gemini rules the lungs. In accidents, the hands, arms, and shoulders, all under Gemini, are most apt to be the points of injury, with the intestines, feet, and thighs the other points through which sickness may work out. On the whole, however, their nerves and yours will give you most of your problems!

Cancer

(JUNE 22–JULY 23)

The Most Sensitive Children of the Zodiac

These children, during early years, are inclined to be somewhat weak physically. Along with their lack of robust health, they show an extremely sensitive emotional nature. They are easily hurt by an unkind word, and so responsive to the conditions around them that they can actually become ill by association with unhealthy or weak nurses or governesses. Because of their affectionate nature, they crave praise and love, but they are slow to show this because of a natural modesty and reticence. There is also a tendency to brood over fancied slights or injuries, more so than will be found in other children. They are, however, extremely unselfish and so lacking in aggressiveness that other children frequently impose upon them. While they are not inclined to fight for their rights and actually feel and fear pain more than less sensitive natures, they have one valuable characteristic which serves well when they are forced to defend themselves—the crab's tenacity and determination to hang on to the bitter end when they have been aroused to defend their rights.

Children born under this sign have a true spirit of patriotism and pride in their country and their home.

You will hear them telling their playmates that their family is the best and their father is the most important man in town, for that's the way they feel about those who are dear to them. They will appreciate their home and stay in it more than most other children.

Do not make many sacrifices to send these children through college unless they show some unusual ability, for their best school is Experience, and they learn more from people, travel, and experience than from any academic education. They will have a natural inclination to travel. And the ups and downs of life which come to most of these children are all lessons that no school could teach. In matters of health, watch their stomachs. Cancer is the sign ruling this part of the body, and unless they rule their stomachs and control their craving for the wrong kind of food, their stomachs will rule—or ruin—them. Don't let them be "fussy" about their meals, but see that they eat plain and nourishing foods and not too much of any kind, for the digestion is inclined to be delicate. Don't expose them to contagious diseases, for they are as receptive to germs as is butter to fish odors when the two are neighbors in the refrigerator. And don't try Spartan methods of discipline, for Cancer children are better ruled by love and encouragement, and will never do their best in an atmosphere of disapproval.

These children are usually mild-mannered and somewhat timid in their reaction to persons other than those with whom they are closely associated. Assurance of acceptance and a feeling of security are very necessary to their well-being. They have a strong attachment to the mother and home, which usually continues throughout life. World activities make an unusually profound impression on these children, who generally are very much in tune with what is taking place on this earthly sphere.

BABIES BORN UNDER THE SIGN OF

Leo

(JULY 24–AUGUST 23)

The Happiest Children of the Zodiac

These children want to be the center of attention—favorable attention, of course. They thrive on adulation; they demand praise for all that they do, and they will do a surprising amount under the stimulus of "That's fine. You are wonderful." They are more responsive to love and tenderness than to punishment. If you find fault with them, they will become irritable and indifferent. As they grow up, that motto of kings, "Noblesse Oblige" (nobility imposes obligation) will bring out the finest qualities in them—nobility, generosity, self-reliance, leadership, pride, and magnanimity.

In talking to them, remember to be exact in your statements and to mean what you say as well as say what you mean, for they not only understand more than many children their age, but they remember your promises. They will tend to imitate the morals and manners of older persons with whom they associate, so pick their companions with care, and see that the books they read are those which preserve the naturally high Leo ideals. They love adventure and their naturally idealistic mind will delight in stories of noble deeds.

They are natural organizers, delighting in positions

of responsibility, and their good nature and ability to mix will fit them for many lines of work in which they contact the public. They are not natural students or very much inclined toward hard manual work, but the artistic and musical qualities natural to Leo will sometimes produce very successful artists in various lines.

These children will not stoop to low or mean action, even at great profit to themselves. No sacrifice is too great for them to make for anyone they love. They act from motives of the heart, not the brain, and are quickly moved by an emotional appeal. They are better leaders than followers; and in children's games, you may have to watch them to see that they do not insist upon leading the game all the time, to their ultimate unpopularity with the gang. Also, do not believe all that they tell you. Their tales have the basis of truth, and they do not lie deliberately, but this inclination will add four more inches on the distance they can jump or a grand aspect to anything they have done.

While these children are quick-tempered, they are equally quick to forgive and their magnanimous nature makes them willing to apologize readily and forgive and forget. They have no bitter enemies, for their hearts seldom find room for hate.

Do not expect them to save their pennies, for theirs is not a saving nature, and their natural tendency to be overoptimistic leads them to think that more pennies will be forthcoming, so they share what they have with the less fortunate with a lordly indifference to the future.

They have unusual vitality; under ordinary conditions, they are seldom sick. There is some tendency to heart trouble, since Leo rules the heart, and to disorders of the blood and some conditions affecting the spine, but on the whole their health is robust and their disposition delightful.

Virgo

(AUGUST 24–SEPTEMBER 23)

The Most Ambitious Children of the Zodiac

Virgo children, above all others, should be given every opportunity for a thorough and complete education. Otherwise, when they grow up, they will be very unhappy to find themselves less equipped mentally than those with whom they associate. They have a natural thirst for knowledge and put great stress upon little things—upon saying the right things and doing the right things—right, for them, meaning correct rather than ethical.

These children have an interest in any subject which they take up and study for the sheer pleasure of acquiring knowledge. They make high grades in school, give the teachers little or no trouble, but may be unknown to most of their schoolmates because of their indifferences to companions and their lack of inclination to "mix" with their fellow students. They are not inclined to seek leadership in games or to push themselves forward for class offices; and while almost always good students, they will tend to remain in the background socially because of lack of interest in making friends.

Order and routine are natural and pleasing to them, and you will never need to complain that they don't pick up their clothes or put away their books or keep their rooms in order. On the other hand, they will probably make everyone who associates with them miserable by insisting that they keep things in the same neat fashion that is second nature to them.

The tendency to be critical of those who are less perfect in behavior than themselves, and to find fault with all the smaller sins and shortcomings of humanity, is one of the worst characteristics to be found in Virgo children. Their motto, whether they are old enough to express it or not, is "Trifles make perfection, but perfection is no trifle," but in their effort to attain it they are inclined "to strain at gnats and swallow camels," as the saying goes. They put so much stress upon small matters that they are unprepared to meet the larger issues, and small disappointments loom so huge in their mind that they are hardly prepared to meet the real tragedies that come into every life at some time. Try, if possible, to develop their sense of proportion in life, and to overcome their natural tendency to be fussy and fretful about trifles.

These children will appreciate a good environment. They are inclined to want to better themselves both socially and financially, and will work hard if they see that their efforts will be rewarded. Diet, hygiene, and science are subjects that interest them.

While they are somewhat quick-tempered and "fussy," they are not inclined to fight, and they seldom act upon anything without deliberation and forethought. They are, therefore, less likely to get into difficulties than the more impulsive and aggressive children.

As far as illness goes, intestinal complaints are the chief causes of poor health, but never let them get into the habit of thinking themselves invalids, for they can "enjoy poor health" to a remarkable degree, and actually intensify their condition by worrying about it.

BABIES BORN UNDER THE SIGN OF

Libra

(SEPTEMBER 24–OCTOBER 23)

The Most Intuitive Children of the Zodiac

These children, more than any others, show artistic tendencies at an early age. They are graceful and attractive when children of other signs are awkward and self-conscious. They are the ones who are called upon by a fond teacher to sing solos on the last day of school or draw the cover of the school magazine, and their popularity is such that less attractive and fortunate children "turn green with envy." There is a reason for this popularity beyond their ability to "show off" to advantage in any artistic field. They are extremely easy to get along with; and in association with children of stronger will, they can be counted on to give in and let the others have things their way—which, of course, makes for popularity. It is, however, an undesirable quality for future development, for above everything else, they need to develop will power—the will to stick to whatever they start until they have made a success of it. Therefore, begin early in life to impress them with the fact that success in any field, artistic or otherwise, is one-third talent and two-thirds the will power to stick to whatever they start until they get to the top. In other words, don't let them be dilettantes who fritter away talents and accomplishments that might be a source of livelihood in life.

They have a natural apathy which is not far from being actual indolence, unless it is overcome in early life. They like to slide through life as easily as possible; and when work interferes with pleasure they are more than willing to sidetrack the work.

In spite of the fact that Venus, planet of the emotions, is the ruler of Libra, these children are not especially responsive to affection and are apt to appear cold and indifferent to the attention of admirers. They are lovable, have a pleasing way about them, but they lack the fighting qualities which they need to make a place for themselves in the world.

If you should find that Libra children want to become dancers when you want them to become schoolteachers or bookkeepers, you will be wise to give up the idea of fitting "square pegs into round holes" and instead give them every encouragement to become a success in the career of their choice. Just see to it that they stick to the career for which they are best suited. The enthusiasm with which they start out is not always a guarantee that the absorbing interest will continue, for they are ardent in anything they do—until something else attracts them, and they switch their energy into a new field.

This changing enthusiasm is no less a characteristic of Libra children than the tendency to swing from the heights of optimism to the depths of melancholy without any adequate reason. While Libra is represented by the balance or scales, the tendency is to swing to extremes in seeking that balance, and Libra is perhaps more marked in these changing moods than any other sign.

They are quick-tempered, but not inclined to hold spite. The danger is that they will become too pliant. Will power and stick-to-itiveness are the qualities they will need most of all.

BABIES BORN UNDER THE SIGN OF

Scorpio

(OCTOBER 24–NOVEMBER 22)

The Most Thorough Children of the Zodiac

Children born under this sign of the zodiac will put the worried parent in the same spot as the driver of a dynamite truck. If you get it where it is going, it may be usefully employed blasting out rocks and destroying outmoded structures, to make way for other finer new developments. If you don't and another truck crashes into it and explodes it prematurely, the resulting damage is terrible to contemplate. "Dynamic"—akin to dynamite in its explosive power—is the word often associated with Scorpio personalities. These children must have, somewhere or somehow, constructive outlets for the energy they possess, or they will, at the most inopportune moment, explode with destructive force which, as often as not, takes shape in physical violence.

Moderation is a word that is practically unknown to these children; and half measures, to them, are worse than none. They are either all for something or someone, or so bitterly against it that no force or argument can sway them. They are natural fighters, always ready to take up an argument either on their own behalf or for some less aggressive comrade to whom they have given their loyalty. Their motto is never "Peace at any price"

—rather it is "War on any provocation." If they are not in physical conflict for material gain, they are in verbal conflict for a cause which they believe to be right.

They can be sarcastic in speech and display a quick-flashing temper, so it is essential in early life to take them in hand and teach them self-control. This will not be an easy task, for they have an unusual amount of determination and do not obey without knowing the reason for doing so. Reason with them and treat them as companions, not as inferiors, and you will find them responsive and loyal. The more straightforward and frank you are in your relations with them, the better you will be able to handle them and the more they will respect you.

Selfishness and self-preservation are dominant Scorpio characteristics, so you need not worry that these children will not be able to look out for themselves and get their share of the world's goods—and a part of the other fellow's share, usually. A shrewd and penetrating mentality makes them quick and intelligent students, especially skilled in mechanical matters.

An unusual amount of physical energy, great recuperative power, and a robust constitution make these children recover quickly from feverish illnesses. Care should be taken in teaching them sex hygiene, as the Sun in Scorpio stimulates the generative and eliminative functions and necessitates unusual moral and physical cleanliness. Sex is very frequently a problem with them, and it is the wise parent who approaches the matter honestly, intelligently, and early. These children lose their illusions about the stork almost as soon as they learn that there is no Santa Claus, so you might as well face the fact and provide an intelligent explanation for them.

Sagittarius

(NOVEMBER 23–DECEMBER 21)

The Most Independent Children of the Zodiac

These children are not only hopeful and trusting, but gay and light of heart. High-mindedness, truthfulness, and a natural lack of selfishness are some of the finer qualities which may be expected of them. They are not, however, natural students or much inclined to sit quietly indoors and read. They would rather be outdoors— riding, skating, sledding, or engaged in some active sport. Try to see to it that they are never without pets of some kind, for living "playthings" are much more to their liking than inanimate toys.

Don't blanket their natural enthusiasm, for it is a quality worthy of cultivation; but direct it, if you wish, along constructive and useful channels. You might be wise to teach them, before they learn from painful experience, that they are not to believe all that they hear, as their own truthful nature makes them believe that everyone with whom they deal will be just as honest. They are slow to understand that others are less honest and aboveboard than they would be in like circumstances. They judge others by their own high standards, and they lack suspiciousness because they have none of the qualities which arouse it in themselves. In your own relations with them, show appreciation of their trustworthiness by giving them all possible freedom. Make chums or companions of them instead of giving them military orders, for they are hard to drive but easy to guide. In the matter of education, let them follow their own inclinations, for their ambitions may range from the ministry through law, or into work that brings them in contact with horses, dogs, and various types of sports.

They will have more than the usual amount of childish curiosity, also, and they will not only ask many questions but may be very analytical and critical of the shortcomings of their family group. Needless to say, such outspoken opinions could be very upsetting, so don't try to stand too much on your dignity with these children. They will obey readily enough if they feel that your request is fair, and your explanation to them is truthful. Their tendency to tease, however, is a habit that should be curbed early in life, as it becomes increasingly annoying as they grow older. Another bad habit is that of making promises in an effort to please and then failing to keep them. Patience is a virtue which they will need to cultivate, since they seldom have it, but on the whole, their faults are minor ones.

Derangement of the nervous system which results from the habit of living too actively is one of the illnesses from which they may suffer, and accidents to the hips (governed by Sagittarius), hands, and joints are not unusual. Their unusual amount of reserve force, however, gives better than average health. One of the best ways to keep them well is to allow them to indulge their natural enthusiasms, for suppression and restriction are both mentally and physically harmful to them.

TRADITIONAL
BIRTHSTONES
of
THE ZODIAC

Capricorn .... Ruby, Chalcedony
Aquarius .... Garnet, Amethyst
Pisces .... Amethyst
Aries .... Bloodstone, Crystal
Taurus .... Sapphire, Ruby, Diamond
Gemini .... Agate, Sapphire, Quartz
Cancer .... Emerald, Cat's-eye, Moonstone
Leo .... Onyx, Amber, Topaz, Tourmaline
Virgo .... Carnelian, Jade, Magnetic Stones
Libra .... Peridot, Aquamarine, Garnet
Scorpio .... Topaz
Sagittarius .... Emerald, Topaz

TRADITIONAL FLOWERS *of* THE ZODIAC

Capricorn .... Flaxweed, Moss, Rush, Ivy, Amaranth
Aquarius .... Daffodil, Pansy
Pisces .... Tuberose, Water Lily, Lotus
Aries .... Buttercup, Daisy, Starthistle
Taurus .... Cowslip, Daisy, Goldenrod, Violet
Gemini .... Marigold, Fern, Lily-of-the-Valley
Cancer .... Iris, Lily, White Poppy, White Rose
Leo .... Poppy, Peony, Sunflower, Red Rose
Virgo ...... Fern, Lavender, Azalea, Morning Glory
Libra ...... Goldenrod, Violet, Cowslip, Nasturtium
Scorpio .. Thistle, Hawthorn, Honeysuckle, Anemone
Sagittarius .... Holly, Jessamine, Carnation,
Chrysanthemum

TRADITIONAL COLORS *of* THE ZODIAC

Capricorn .... Dark Browns, Green, Black
Aquarius .... Mingled Shades, Stripes, Plaids
Pisces .... Green-Blue, Shades of Lavender, Amethyst
Aries .... Brilliant Red
Taurus .... Red-Orange, Yellow, Cream
Gemini ...... Mixed and Spotted, Silvery Gray, Blue
Cancer .... Delicate Greens, Pearl, Opalescent Shades
Leo .... Amber, Deep Orange, Golden Yellows
Virgo .... Yellow, Grayish Blue
Libra ... Pale Blue to Deep Blue, Pale Yellow, Pastels
Scorpio .... Deep Red
Sagittarius .... Rich Deep Violet-Blue